consumer guide
to used and surplus
home appliances and
furnishings

# consumer guide
# to used and surplus
# home appliances and
# furnishings

### PATRICIA WILSON
University of Washington

HOUGHTON MIFFLIN COMPANY · BOSTON

Atlanta · Dallas · Geneva, Illinois
Hopewell, New Jersey · Palo Alto

*To my husband, Chester, without whom*
*this book could not have been written.*

OCT 3 73

Printed in the U.S.A.

Library of Congress Catalog Card Number: 72-11623

ISBN: 0-395-15049-3

# contents

1775533

# preface

The Consumer Guide to Used and Surplus Home Appliances and Furnishings was written for use in home equipment, consumer economics, and family economics courses. It's also well suited for use in extension programs and in adult education work in the home economics area.

The only consumer education references available up to now have dealt with the new market, while demand has increased for specific buying guidelines for the growing used and surplus appliances and furnishings market.

Knowing where to shop for these items is important. The numerous sources frequently differ to some degree in quality of merchandise, price, service, and reliability; but, nationally, certain similarities seem widespread. These are outlined in the Guide.

In researching for the book, I checked retail outlets in cities across the country, pricing appliances and furnishings. I also evaluated the quality of the offered goods, formulating a few simple tests and check lists to help the consumer. These are also included in many chapters.

The general buying guidelines given in the Guide are useful in sizing up new merchandise as well as that offered in the used and surplus marketplace. The service life expectancy figures apply in both cases — refer to them when budgeting for appliance replacements, or when comparing the dollar value of secondhand with new goods.

Any appliance, new or used, requires proper maintenance and repair to remain in top working condition. Major work is best left to a competent repairman, but repairs can be expensive, and economy in maintenance goes hand in hand with a good purchase price. Chapter Seven contains instructions for a few routine appliance repairs that the average consumer should be able to handle. Maintenance practices designed to lower utility costs, cut repair bills, and lengthen the useful life of your appliances are also suggested. In addition, many use and care safety precautions are included.

Home furnishings need care, too — we're all faced with an occasional upholstery stain or table top blemish. How often have you wandered around the supermarket aisles, wondering which wax or cleaner would do the job? The Guide tells which.

All successful buying requires product knowledge, buying skill, and a sound understanding of our own special priorities. The wise consumer must evaluate values, goals, and resources before buying to formulate a spending plan designed to help achieve what he or she wants. Chapter 10, "Budgeting for Appliances and Furnishings," is an indispensable aid in this process.

The used home furnishings market has a long and respectable history. Well constructed furniture often passes from generation to generation. Many young families start out with study hand-me-downs from parents' attics. Auctions, another traditional source of low cost appliances and furnishings, today are attended by a wide range of potential buyers. And the recurrent waves of nostalgia for the old or "collectable" will preserve the secondhand and antique furniture shops.

But another, equally important factor is involved here: Americans are increasingly aware of the dwindling supply of natural resources, and are consequently scrutinizing the disposal of everything from soft drink bottles to steel girders. Isn't it also a good idea to recycle appliances and furnishings, instead of disposing of them long before their useful life is over?

If every consumer did this, the mountain of discarded appliances in the nation's junkyards could be razed and, in time, appliance manufacturers could be encouraged to stock needed parts for extended periods of time. The flourishing used car and parts industry shows that the idea has great possibilities.

Different as we all are in our needs, resources, and priorities, the used and surplus market merits our consideration. It offers another alternative in the marketplace, and the wider our choices as consumers, the greater our chances for satisfaction.

—PW

# 1

# the surplus market

The term "surplus" indicates that which is left over when a need is satisfied. Surplus furniture or equipment may be used, damaged, irregular, or simply old. The condition of surplus furnishings ranges from "nearly new" to "frankly useless." While wider variations in quality exist among surplus goods, shopping in the new market requires many of the same consumer decisions. All successful purchasing requires product knowledge and buying skill on the part of the consumer.

To begin learning about the surplus furniture and appliance market, read the classified ads in your local newspaper. You then will start to understand the many reasons for sales and the great diversity of surplus goods available. We find ads that read, "Divorce forces sale, everything must go," "Trade walnut chair and ottoman, like new, for 10-speed bicycle or chain saw," "Refrigerator, never out of crate, $100 off new price," and finally "Washer, needs work, $10." Old furniture becomes "junque" or "collectables" when offered by the imaginative dealer and simply "secondhand" when sold by the plebeian salvage store. Families or dealers advertising used appliances for sale tend to be more factual in their descriptions than those selling furniture, referring mainly to brand, year, and special features of the equipment.

Estimating the actual dollar savings when buying used furniture is more difficult because of the lack of easy objective guidelines and the many variables of furniture design and construction. A more objective method of pricing is evident in the used appliance market. The consumer who thoroughly investigates the surplus offerings and then selects with care can expect to save anywhere from 20 to 90 per cent of the cost of new equipment, depending upon how much work he is willing to do himself.

## Why Buy?

Why turn to the surplus market when buying appliances or furniture for your home? The answer for most of us is simple – to stretch our budget. Whether because of financial need or the general desire for a bargain that exists in most of us, we seek the best possible buy for our dollar. Other valid reasons for purchasing used furniture exist as well. Generally, when decorating our homes, we select furnishings on an individual, style-oriented basis. We strive to develop a certain character or atmosphere. Sometimes the used market satisfies this individualized need more adequately than the current fashion. The true antique market is one such example and the do-it-yourself approach to furnishings is another. Many families explore secondhand shops and visit auctions partly as a form of family recreation and partly because of a changing emphasis in contemporary economic values.

While buying "on time" has become almost a way of life for many, the used market makes it easier for those wishing to buy without paying an added premium for such use of credit. What better source of merchandise for the family with a restricted budget, the newly married couple furnishing their first temporary apartment, or for students away at college? The family equipping a second home or trailer for vacations might also be well advised to check the surplus market. Too, there are instances where a homemaker's work might be facilitated by two appliances, such as an upright and a canister vacuum cleaner. The secondhand market could provide both for the price of a single new cleaner, leaving the family equipment budget intact.

Portable appliances that are used only a few times each year might be more wisely purchased in the surplus market. As an alternate to buying, families sometimes elect to rent some of the equipment, rug scrubbers or floor polishers, for instance, when needed for periodic cleaning jobs. Many hardware and grocery stores offer such equipment on a daily or hourly rental basis. Similarly, large quantity serving appliances such as coffee urns for parties can be rented from caterers or special stores. Some of us borrow from neighbors or relatives when a need arises. However, you just might save money and preserve friendships by checking the newspaper classified ads or visiting a local salvage store instead of renting or borrowing such equipment. For the cost of renting a large coffeemaker just twice, you probably could have bought a used one.

While some portable appliances, like electric roaster-ovens, deep fat fryers, pressure saucepans, and even waffle irons, may not fall within the "seasonal" or "special entertaining" categories, they too might be wisely selected from among the surplus offerings. These may be used infrequently because of family food habits and yet be required on occasion for preparation of a special item. Secondhand models can be found with much service life remaining, at a price that makes their purchase practical even when used infrequently. While admittedly the general secondhand portable appliance offerings differ markedly in appearance from new, such equipment when well chosen can give years of service at low cost. It may be some consolation to remember that many new appliances lose much of their shiny appeal after a few years in your home.

Having considered some of the "whys" of buying, let us discuss a few of the reasons for *selling* used furnishings and equipment. Many consumers have become so oriented to color and style that older appliances and furnishings, even though many years of service remain, are replaced with new. For example, the life expectancy of a refrigerator has been estimated at 16 years, and yet a check of the classified ads will reveal many offered for sale that are not yet 10 years old. A similar desire for change can be seen in the home furnishings field. Greater family mobility, with the accompanying changes of residence, result in home furnishings and appliances used only a year or two being offered for quick sale, often far below general market value. Excessive use of credit adds to this supply as payments become difficult to meet when a family emergency arises. Another source of surplus equipment arises when families move into new homes where kitchen and laundry appliances are provided, and they no longer have a need for their previous furnishings and appliances. Many of the newer appliance models offered for sale come into the market because of this reason.

In general, furniture has a longer life span than appliances, and with care many pieces can be passed on through a family or offered for resale. Changes in the family life cycle may free furniture for such disposition. When the last child has started kindergarten, nursery furniture becomes surplus and is often advertised for sale. The period following the time the last child leaves home frequently signals the redecorating and refurbishing of the family home. While some of the furniture may clearly show signs of age, other pieces after cleaning and some minor repair can be good buys for another family. Retirement marks another period when furnishings may become surplus. When a couple decides to move from a large family home to smaller quarters, they are forced to dispose of certain furnishings.

Care is required every time we make a choice in the marketplace, whether searching for new or used goods. Some knowledge of construction criteria and maintenance needs should precede every purchase for the home. However, the responsibility is more clearly the buyer's when making most purchases through the surplus market. In defense of the used market, we must recognize that it offers us one more alternative to conventional retail sales, and the wider our choice as consumers the greater the chance for satisfaction.

**Where to Buy**

Knowing where to shop for surplus furnishings and appliances is an important consumer consideration. While many sources exist, each differing in quality, price, service, and reliability, there are certain similarities to help guide us. Newspaper classified advertising, bulletin boards found in laundromats, grocery stores, and other private or community facilities all offer goods for sale by private owners. Some furniture and appliance stores offer trade-ins, although more equipment than furniture is sold in this manner. Independent appliance repairmen may recondition and sell used household equipment in addition to providing regular repair services. When well established in the community, they are excellent sources to check for serviceable appliances. To locate these outlets, check your neighborhood newspapers or the telephone directory.

*Classified telephone directory listings.* When looking for surplus equipment or furnishings, the classified section of your telephone directory can save time and steps. Begin by checking the listings under

"Secondhand Stores," "Liquidators," and "Salvage Dealers." Often your least expensive sources of home furnishings and equipment are the salvage stores, including those sponsored by churches, community service, or private organizations. When searching for used furniture, turn to the "Furniture, Used" listing and finally, the "Antique" classification. Antique shops carry attractive, frankly secondhand furnishings at a lesser cost than the title suggests. Look under "Appliances, Used" and "Repairing and Parts" headings for additional equipment resale sources as well as necessary parts and service information when repairs are needed. Within many of these classifications you will find trade and barter-type swap shops, auction houses, and the more conventional secondhand type of store.

*Newspaper classified advertising.*    Person-to-person newspaper classified advertising offers the widest assortment of nearly new furniture and appliances at generally lower prices than other retail outlets. Families mention many reasons for these sales, some true and some more creative. It is well to investigate each buy on its own merits without undue dependence on the owner's salesmanship. In general, private parties price merchandise well below market value. However, the price structure is less consistent than that found in other conventional outlets.

Check the newspaper ads for several weeks before buying, so that you can become familiar with the general price level. This is especially helpful when choosing an appliance, as greater price standardization exists here than in the home furnishings field. When you find an interesting piece of equipment or furniture but the asking price seems out of line, make a counter-offer, leaving your phone number. And should you not hear from the seller within a week, check again. Equitable prices sometimes take time!

*Appliance stores.*    When shopping in an appliance store that offers trade-in equipment for resale, check the guarantee, service, and delivery against that found in other outlets. Often secondhand appliances sold through such stores are accompanied by a 90-day guarantee on parts and/or labor. Be sure to read any guarantee carefully before purchasing as those covering parts *and* labor are more valuable to the consumer than those limited to a parts-only replacement. It always seems that the nonfunctioning part is the inexpensive one, but the labor cost for installation is yet another story. Remember, too, that promises in writing are the only ones that count.

Newspaper ads sometimes refer to equipment that has been "rebuilt" or "reconditioned." Reconditioned appliances have little more than a general cleanup and replacement of parts necessary for *immediate* operation. While the term "rebuilt" indicates a more thorough overhaul, the accuracy of the word is wholly dependent upon dealer reliability. The selection of a reputable dealer who has served the community for some time and who has a record of responsibility to his customers cannot be overrated when making any purchase, whether new or used.

*Secondhand shops.* Secondhand shops are interesting places in which to browse, and sometimes they offer bargains in small appliances and furnishings. The quality of merchandise and the prices vary widely, all the way from "dirty and overpriced" to "clean and economical." Test any appliance before purchasing as, almost without exception, the policy is firmly one of "no refunds or exchanges." When buying furniture, chances of satisfaction are greater because the general condition of goods is more apparent to the consumer than in the case of an appliance. However, whether buying equipment or furnishings in a secondhand store, settle on a reasonable price *before* agreeing to buy as there tends to be some flexibility in many of these outlets, and bargaining may be in order.

*Garage sales, auctions, salvage outlets.* These can be rewarding places to visit budgetwise, but caution is the byword, especially when purchasing appliances. While no guarantees worthy of consideration are offered at garage sales or auctions, a short term exchange privilege is common at many salvage stores. However, greater satisfaction is assured when buying home furnishings than appliances through these outlets as a wide price range and variety of merchandise can be found. While true antiques still can be located through salvage shops and country auctions, exceptional bargains are more difficult to find due to the fact that "antiquing" has now become such a popular avocation. Most salvage shops have a resource person, often a volunteer, who screens contributions for potential antique value.

The major sources of supply for salvage shops are families who are disposing of surplus items from their homes. While some appliances and furnishings have years of service remaining, others might better have been sent directly to the city dump. In rarer instances, manufacturers who discourage markdowns may prefer to send merchandise not moving through conventional retail stores to a salvage outlet operated by a charitable organization, thus claiming a tax deduction.

Whenever possible, test any appliances or furniture found in salvage shops before purchase regardless of the return policy. This suggestion becomes increasingly important when selecting heavy major appliances that require a trailer and several strong friends to unload. While the condition of furniture is easier to determine than that of appliances, do take time to check each piece carefully. Remove drawers, turn chairs upside down, and generally inspect the important construction features necessary for long service.

Finance companies, contrary to popular image, are reluctant to reclaim furniture and appliances because of the costs involved and the comparatively low resale value. While more difficult to locate, such goods when available can be good buys. The county clerk's office will often furnish information concerning specific merchandise on the bankruptcy court docket. A telephone call can save time and steps. Local auction houses frequently dispose of goods repossessed by finance companies as well as those involved in estate settlements. Household moving and storage firms also hold auctions to dispose of unclaimed personal effects when storage fees become delinquent. Generally, these are irregularly scheduled on the mover's premises. A word of caution when attending auctions might be to arrive early before the bidding starts so that you can check thoroughly any furniture or equipment of interest before making your bid. It is always a good idea whenever attending an auction to mentally set a firm price limit ahead of time, as even the most sophisticated buyer can suffer a touch of "auction fever" during the spirited bidding. While offering perhaps less general recreation, sealed bid auctions protect the buyer from his own enthusiasm during open bidding and, in this respect, have some merits that are often overlooked.

*Freight damaged appliances.* Another category you may wish to consider that differs somewhat from the secondhand equipment market is that of freight damaged appliances. The defects vary in severity from a few scratches to more serious mechanical or electrical problems. Before buying this equipment, examine all problem areas to determine the extent of the damage and to ascertain the required repairs, if any. It is not uncommon to find water heaters, marked down 25 per cent because of scratches that may be completely hidden during installation, that are still covered by the original guarantee.

While freight damaged equipment can be found in any store, certain surplus outlets specialize in such goods. Your classified telephone directory can offer assistance here. Newspaper classified ads that read "still in the original crate" or "never used" usually refer to surplus goods of some type. Such appliances may be freight damaged models or older equipment that did not sell. At times, slightly damaged appliances are worth looking into if you have shopped the new market and are familiar enough with current prices to make a cost comparison.

*Dealer demonstration models, previous year, and special sale merchandise.*  While appliance sales occurring at the time of a manufacturer's model change are perhaps more predictable than furniture clearances, department stores generally run home furnishings sales during the months of February and August. However, during the rest of the year you may find special sales which sometimes include slightly damaged or soiled furnishings. Always consider the cost of necessary repairs or cleaning as part of the original price. When purchasing "irregulars" or "seconds," be sure that any flaws can be tolerated by your family. Many bargains turn into liabilities because of failure to consider this. Compare prices of similar quality regular merchandise before buying such goods.

Be sure any markdown represents a true saving. A reputable dealer is the best insurance against fictitious pre-ticketing to make subsequent markdowns more appealing to the unwary buyer. However, sound knowledge of the general market is a consumer's greatest asset when making any purchase. When possible, plan purchases in the used market to coincide with general furnishings or appliance sales. When a family purchases a new refrigerator during the special white goods sale period, it frequently will have an older appliance to trade in or sell. See the Shopping Calendar in Chapter 10 for general sale periods.

When in doubt about the exact year of an appliance, check the model and serial number. A call to a local distributor, manufacturer's sales department, or factory representative will answer your question. Normally, the very act of asking for this information tends to refresh a seller's mind concerning appliance age. A two-year-old washer sitting unused in a dealer's showroom has many years of life remaining, but the buyer has a right to know that it *is* two years old rather than year-end merchandise or "this year's demonstration model."

**Low Cost Alternatives**

One final suggestion when shopping for inexpensive home furnishings is to consider the do-it-yourself field. Even though it is outside the realm of used or surplus merchandise, no book on low cost home furnishings would be complete without a word about furniture you can build yourself or complete after some initial factory construction. Unfinished furniture is a good buy and an excellent choice in many situations. However, at least consider the price of the finishing supplies, if not your labor, when computing the total cost.

Before attempting any project, weigh your own talent and individual demand for perfection. We all have different personal values and what is one family's prize possession may be another's junk. With a bit of time and patience, an unfinished door can be transformed into a desk, a coffee table, the bottom of a sofa, or with a foam pad, a guest bed. Boards and concrete blocks or bricks can substitute for bookcases, a room divider, or other storage arrangement. While not the answer for every family, the combination of such self-designed furnishings, supplemented by a few well chosen pieces, can create a comfortable and attractive home. All it takes is imagination and the ability to sand, paint, and wield a hammer.

# 2

# general appliance considerations

Surplus appliances can offer years of service to families at low cost, but some work on the consumer's part is necessary to ensure satisfaction. Before buying:

First, jot down all the features you *need* as well as those desirable but deferrable. Take this reminder with you when shopping and refer to it often, as successful purchasing is based upon consideration of your own values balanced against available resources.

Next, check several sources of supply, listing appliance features, service, guarantee, price, and any other important considerations. Start by investigating the classified newspaper ads for several weeks to gain a knowledge of the surplus market.

Finally, whenever possible, try before you buy! Don't be afraid to remove appliance covers and drawers or inspect elements and electrical connections for wear or damage. Check refrigeration and freezing compartments with a thermometer. Minutes spent at this point will save hours (and dollars) later in repairs.

**Need, Storage, and Utility Capacity**

Ask yourself a few questions before buying any new or used appliance:

Do I really need this appliance? To answer, it is well to question the number of times an appliance will be used in the home and the amount of satisfaction it will bring.

Is sufficient storage space available? Generally we measure the space required for major pieces of equipment quite carefully. However, this is often not the case when purchasing small appliances. Countless portables gather dust on top shelves because access is inconvenient for the homemaker. Convenient storage near the work center is necessary for maximum satisfaction.

Will the appliance duplicate the work of equipment already in the home? Basically, the range oven can handle the same meal preparation jobs that a portable oven-broiler does. A well constructed knife cuts in much the same way as the electric powered one. An electric frypan pops corn, cooks pancakes, simmers and heats rolls in addition to frying. The frypan actually eliminates the need for an electric corn popper, griddle, saucepan and portable bun warmer and yet we frequently find all of these appliances in a single kitchen. As consumers, we seem to buy more portables than we actually need. However, it is difficult to define a "need," and each of us must evaluate our own based upon individual values and resources.

Am I willing to assume the work that accompanies this purchase? Perhaps you really do not want to scrub your own carpeting but would rather continue to have it cleaned professionally. In that case, you have little need for an electric rug scrubber. It would actually create more work for you rather than lightening your load. If your concern is for the money-saving aspect of shampooing your own carpeting, then your decision may well be different. And if your family is satisfied with frozen waffles, there may be little need for a waffle baker.

Do I have enough money to make the purchase at this time? When we borrow money to buy anything, we are adding an additional cost to the goods. When we elect to investigate the surplus equipment market, we are in a way attempting to avoid some of these credit costs. In addition to initial costs, the added expense of maintenance and operation must be added to any appliance purchase. It is well to consider how the total expenditure will fit into the family budget at a specific time. If this is questionable, you must judge whether the immediate need is great or if the purchase can be postponed until funds are more readily available. While used or surplus equipment costs less than new, it is far from free. Furthermore, any purchase carries some risk and the chance or repair expense always remains to a degree.

Is adequate electricity, gas or water available? In some instances the cost of installing a dishwasher has exceeded the purchase price because utilities were inconveniently located or cabinet and counter renovation was necessary.

A wise consumer checks electrical capacity, placement of outlets, venting facilities, and plumbing before buying in order to avoid additional costs that the family budget cannot bear. Check the availability of 240 volt special purpose circuits for electric ranges, hot water heaters, and clothes dryers. While some dryers can be adapted to use 120 volt power, this is fairly unsatisfactory for all except the small portable dryers. This lower voltage level generally adds two and a half to three times the drying time required when using a 240 volt circuit hookup. This not only amounts to extra operational cost but greatly increases the length of time required to complete the family wash. Check to see that plumbing hookups and drainage facilities for clothes washers, water heaters, and dishwashers are available before purchase.

**Appliance Manuals**

Ideally, the original use and care manual should accompany any equipment purchased, but in the case of a secondhand model frequently the previous owner has long since lost or misplaced this invaluable reference. While possibly less of a problem with many portable appliances, the absence of vital installation and service information can cause great difficulty when major appliances are purchased. Should the time come when you are selling rather than buying a used appliance, you will notice that the top market price is more easily obtainable when original sales information and owner's manual accompany the equipment. If repairs have been made, an itemized and dated bill for the work and parts will be welcomed by the prospective buyer.

A number of appliance manufacturers were queried to determine whether manuals for older models were still available. Most companies assured us that they would duplicate instructions from their files in cases where the original copies were unavailable. While this may not always be the case, it is well first to check the original manufacturer when you need a use and care manual. If the firm fails to fulfill your request, another source to check, especially when inquiring about a major appliance, is your local utility home economist. She often maintains a file of instruction booklets to help answer the many customer inquiries concerning appliance use and maintenance. As a last resort, salvage outlets sometimes sell old use and care manuals very inexpensively. The chances of locating one for a particular appliance model are slim, but a telephone call to inquire may be worth your effort.

## Service Life Expectancy

The forecast life expectancy of appliances depends upon many variables. Amount of use, care in installation, maintenance, product design, and even geographic location of the home play a part in determining this elusive statistic. In view of these variables, manufacturers are somewhat reluctant to indicate service life estimates for household equipment. The Association of Home Appliance Manufacturers (AHAM) has suggested a ten-year appliance write-off when budgeting for new equipment purchases.[1]

More specific (although older) guidelines for service life expectancy have been established by Pennock and Jaeger (see Table 2–1). However, the appliance industry generally agrees on the validity of these original figures, and they are quoted widely in consumer publications.

A survey of equipment offered for sale through classified newspaper ads and secondhand outlets indicates that first owners trade in appliances earlier than necessary from a service life standpoint. While it may be that the life expectancy estimates are optimistic in today's market, based on the estimate of appliance retailers, it seems apparent that the desire for new features, styling, and in some cases capacity motivates most consumers. A careful look at the personal classified offerings tends to substantiate this view.

## Repair Service and Parts

When purchasing any appliance, new or used, it is always wise to consider availability of service unless you are handy with tools and have more than the average amount of basic electrical knowledge. Purchasing

[1]Guenther Baumgart, "Consumers Are Our Best Friends," *The Year of the Consumer* (Chicago: Association of Home Appliance Manufacturers, 1970), p. 8.

**TABLE 2–1**

*Service life expectancy under one owner of selected items of household equipment*[2]

| Item and Collection Date* | New When Acquired | | Used When Acquired | |
|---|---|---|---|---|
| | Service Life Expectancy (years) | Standard Error † (per cent) | Service Life Expectancy (years) | Standard Error † (per cent) |
| Washing machines, electric: | | | | |
| Automatic and semi-automatic | | | | |
| December 1957 | 11 | 10 | 5 | 15 |
| January 1957 | 9 | 10 | 5 | 14 |
| Wringer and spin-dryer | | | | |
| December 1957 | 10 | 10 | 6 | 11 |
| January 1957 | 9 | 10 | 5 | 10 |
| Clothes dryers, electric | | | | |
| May 1961 | 14 | 21 | – | – |
| Refrigerators, electric | | | | |
| May 1960 | 16 | 8 | 8 | 11 |
| January 1957 | 15 | 8 | 8 | 10 |
| Freezers | | | | |
| May 1961 | 15 | 11 | 11 | 21 |
| Ranges | | | | |
| Electric | | | | |
| June 1959 | 16 | 12 | 8 | 13 |
| January 1957 | 15 | 12 | 6 | 14 |
| Gas | | | | |
| June 1959 | 16 | 10 | 9 | 12 |
| January 1957 | 15 | 10 | 8 | 12 |
| Vacuum cleaners | | | | |
| Upright | | | | |
| December 1957 | 18 | 14 | 8 | 15 |
| Tank | | | | |
| December 1957 | 15 | 12 | – | – |
| Sewing machines | | | | |
| Electric | | | | |
| June 1959 | 24 | 13 | 16 | 17 |
| Treadle | | | | |
| June 1959 | – | – | 13 | 12 |

| Item and Collection Date* | New When Acquired | | Used When Acquired | |
|---|---|---|---|---|
| | Service Life Expectancy (years) | Standard Error† (per cent) | Service Life Expectancy (years) | Standard Error† (per cent) |
| Toasters | | | | |
| Automatic | | | | |
| June 1959 | 15 | 8 | 8 | 15 |
| Non-automatic | | | | |
| June 1959 | 7 | 15 | 4 | 16 |

*Date from this study on television sets, living room rugs, and automobiles is omitted here. Collection dates are dates when data was collected.

[2] Jean L. Pennock, Carol M. Jaeger, "Household Service Life of Durable Goods," *Journal of Home Economics,* 56, No. 1 (January, 1964), 23.

†Standard error of the service life expectancy expressed as percentage of the service life expectancy.

any equipment is especially risky when the manufacturer has ceased production completely or discontinued the specific line of appliances in question. Regardless of what equipment you plan to purchase, you should consider the advantages of selecting among well known and reliable brands.

Lack of those repair parts actually necessary for operation can pose quite a problem when trouble occurs. While many parts are interchangeable among models, there are instances where replacements are almost impossible to find. One source to investigate is the independent appliance repairman, who often stocks parts long after manufacturers have discontinued production. In larger cities, check the classified section of the telephone directory under "Electric Appliances, Repairing and Parts" for an appliance parts distributor who ordinarily stocks parts for most major manufacturers' equipment. These distributors are good sources for parts needed to repair a variety of appliances. While there, ask for a catalog which will serve as a valuable future reference.

In August, 1971, AHAM's board of directors recommended to its member manufacturers that service parts should be available for both new and older major appliances still in general use and in adequate supply so that 95 per cent of all orders received from repair services or parts distributors could be shipped within two business days and the remainder within two weeks except in rare cases. They further stated that parts and service for older models should be available as long as reasonable demand exists considering date of production, whether the part was functional or decorative, and the experienced frequency of failure for each part.[3]

However, several of the manufacturers consulted later stocked the vital parts up to fifteen years after model discontinuation while others carried renewal parts for less than five years. Therefore, when purchasing a major appliance, it would seem particularly important to check the availability of functional parts. An appliance parts distributor's catalog is one readily available source of such information. Adaptations for out-of-stock parts can be made, but a certain mechanical skill and some special tools are required. As a general rule, more interchangeable parts are available for making repairs on older portable appliances. Heating element replacements, for example, can be found in many hardware stores.

Industrial surplus yards and salvage shops often carry spare parts for a variety of appliance repair needs. To save money, become familiar with these sources of supply before such a need arises. Many carry ice cube trays, appliance cords, electric frypan covers, mixer beaters, and wringer washer rollers — each for under one dollar. These, as well as broiler pans, racks for ranges, refrigerator shelves, and other miscellaneous appliance parts, have been taken from dismantled equipment that was not considered profitable to repair and offer for resale.

## Simple Test Equipment

Before buying, check the operation of secondhand appliances whenever possible. Surprisingly enough, even the most non-mechanically oriented consumer can spot many weaknesses that indicate the probability of future problems. Noise, vibration, lack of temperature control, or a laboring motor can be detected by all of us, if we only take the time to really stop, look, and listen. Going beyond this basic level of observation, a few very simple, easy-to-use test instruments can increase the probability of making a wise appliance selection.

*Continuity testlight.* When an electrical outlet is unavailable for testing equipment under actual use conditions, two common problems

---

[3]AHAM Recommendations to Consumers for Availability of Major Appliance Parts and Service Literature." (Approved by AHAM's Board of Directors, August 11, 1971, private communications from AHAM, Chicago.)

that may go undetected in an appliance are grounded circuits and open circuits. A continuity testlight that uses flashlight batteries can be helpful in detecting either of these conditions. Since you are exposed to the same minimal voltage found in any flashlight when making this test, it is entirely safe and should not be confused with that of checking "live" electric circuits which admittedly requires greater care and knowledge. The continuity testlight shown in Figure 2–1 can be purchased inexpensively at most hardware stores. Use it to locate circuit trouble in all your home appliances and cordsets. In addition, you can check continuity of fuses, sockets, switches, and spark plugs that appear to be defective.

When an exposed internal electric circuit comes in contact with the metal housing of an appliance either through a break in insulation or other accidental means, the exterior metal parts of the appliance become electrically "live." The user becomes an unwilling part of this circuit when contact is made and receives an electric shock. When testing for these accidental grounds within an appliance circuit:

1. Disconnect the appliance from its electric outlet. NEVER WORK ON A LIVE CIRCUIT WITH THIS TESTLIGHT.
2. If the appliance has a switch, turn it to the "on" position.
3. Touch the spring clip or lead wire from the testlight to one prong of the appliance plug.
4. Touch the metal body of the continuity testlight to an exposed metal section of the appliance being tested. When using the homemade testlight shown on pages 18-23, use the second lead wire rather than the flashlight body for this test.
5. Repeat steps 3 and 4, attaching the clip or wire to the second prong of the appliance plug.

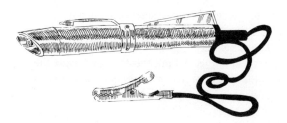

Figure 2–1 *Continuity testlight*

If the testlight bulb glows when trying either prong, the appliance circuit is defective and current is leaking into the appliance housing. Such a condition can result in a serious or even lethal shock for the user depending upon conditions of use. In any event, the appliance must be repaired BEFORE you can use it safely. In some cases, this is a very simple process requiring no more than insulation repair on existing wires. In other instances, the repair may be complicated by the existence of a broken part.

The second common appliance problem you may encounter is a lack of continuity, which indicates an open circuit. When this happens, electric current cannot flow through the complete appliance circuit, and the appliance will not operate until proper repairs have been made. Before testing any appliance, check to see that the switching device is turned to the "on" position. In the case of the pop-up toaster, be sure the bread carriage is down in order to close the circuit. When checking an electric range where many circuits exist (one for each surface element, broiler, and oven), check each in turn by switching one selector knob or button to "on" at a time, repeating the test at the appliance cord prongs for each circuit in turn. Switch to "off" before testing the next circuit.

Check for continuity of circuit as follows:

1. Disconnect the appliance from its electric outlet.
2. Turn the switching device to the "on" position.
3. Touch the spring clip or test lead of the continuity testlight to one prong of the appliance plug, as shown in Figure 2—2.
4. Touch the metal case of the tester to the other prong of the appliance plug, as shown in Figure 2—2. (For this test, ignore the appliance plug ground prong if present.)

If the testlight glows, circuit continuity exists. This test is valid for most major and portable appliances. However, it is VERY IMPORTANT that all appliances are completely disconnected from electricity before testing. The switches or temperature dial should be in the "on" position and refrigerators or freezers must not be set at "defrost." Do not buy any appliance that lacks circuit continuity. The equipment will not work until repaired, and while this is usually possible, the task is difficult if not impossible for anyone without electrical experience and the proper tools.

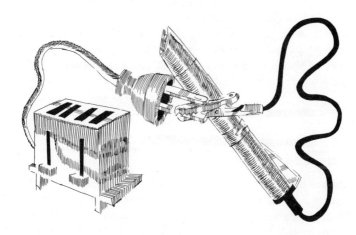

**Figure 2—2** *Testing for circuit continuity*

If you wish to *make* rather than purchase your own continuity testlight, two methods of construction are given below. Using the first method, an ordinary flashlight can be converted to serve the same purposes as the commercially available testlight without any tools whatsoever. The second testlight construction requires the use of a small drill and perhaps a soldering iron. While this method results in the more secure construction, it does involve permanent alteration of a flashlight. Either can be used for the same tests as the commercially available continuity testlight with one variation: with the homemade versions, the second lead wire serves the purpose of the testlight body on the commercial model.

SUPPLIES REQUIRED FOR TESTLIGHT #1

Flashlight with metal case or metal switch if enclosed in plastic
Two- to three-inch by one-inch rectangles of heavy-duty aluminum foil
2 rectangles of waxed paper, slightly wider than aluminum foil (needed
     only when metal-bodied flashlight is used)
1 yard of bell wire
Masking, cloth, or plastic tape to secure wires around flashlight (optional)

CONSTRUCTION DIRECTIONS

1. Cut bell wire into two lengths, each 18 inches long.
2. Strip seven inches of insulation from one end of both wires using a knife, scissors, or wire stripper.  Strip 3/4 inch of insulation from the opposite end of both wires.  When completed you will have two wires each with seven inches of bare copper exposed at one end and 3/4 inch exposed on the opposite end.

3/4 inch                                    7 inches

3. Remove the reflector from the flashlight.  Insert aluminum foil rectangles behind the reflector on both sides of the case as shown. When using a metal-bodied flashlight, place a piece of waxed paper approximately 1/4 inch wider than foil underneath each foil rectangle to insulate the aluminum from the metal body.

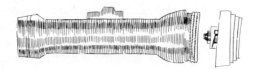

4. Hold reflector tightly against the foil by pressing against the lens with a finger while the cap is gently screwed in place.
5. Wrap the seven-inch exposed section of one wire firmly around the flashlight securing both pieces of aluminum foil as indicated.  Twist the end tightly around top portion of exposed wire to ensure a good contact.

6. The remaining wire, stripped of insulation as described in (2), above, should be wrapped around the metal flashlight body or over the metal switch cover as shown. Twist the end of the wire tightly around top portion of exposed wire to secure.

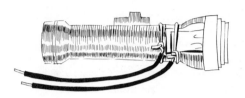

7. Masking, plastic, or cloth tape can be wrapped around the flashlight case to protect the wire, if desired. A shock hazard is not involved in this low voltage instance so less stringent insulation is required than that called for in much other test equipment; therefore, electrician's tape is not required.

8. The loose ends of both wires are your test terminals. Check your testlight for continuity by touching both leads together as shown. If the flashlight glows, you are ready for the next step, that of checking appliances.

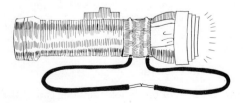

SUPPLIES REQUIRED FOR TESTLIGHT #2

Flashlight with metal case or metal switch if enclosed in plastic
1 yard bell wire
Sufficient masking, cloth, or plastic tape to secure the wires (optional)
Small drill
Soldering iron or 2 self-tapping screws

CONSTRUCTION DIRECTIONS

1. Dismantle the flashlight.
2. Drill a hole about 1/8 inch or slightly larger through the case directly in back of reflector as shown.  Check to make sure you do not
   drill into the switch contact inside case.

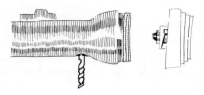

3. Cut bell wire in half.  Using one of these wires, strip three inches of
   insulation from one end.  Insert this bare wire through the hole
   drilled, securing it to the reflector or metal ring into which the
   reflector is mounted by either soldering or inserting a self-tapping
   screw and then twisting the wire around the head.

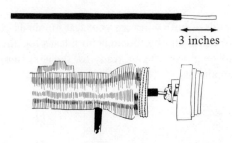

3 inches

4. Next, remove 1/4 inch of insulation from one end of the second
   wire.  Fasten this bare portion of the wire to the metal body of the

flashlight. If a plastic covered light has been used the wire should be fastened to the metal switch. When the case or switch is brass or steel, a fast connection can be made by soldering. However, if these parts are aluminum or another alloy, connect by drilling a hole and then inserting a self-tapping screw to hold the twisted wire securely.

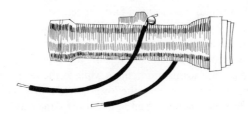

5. After assembling the testlight, the wires may be reinforced by wrapping with two or three turns of tape as shown.

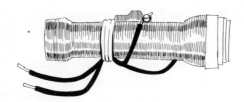

6. Remove insulation from the last 1/2 inch of each wire. These are your test terminals. When not in use, be sure they do not touch each other or the metal portion of the case. Should this happen, the battery will eventually discharge and the cells will have to be replaced.

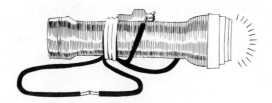

*Homemade "stethoscope."* When shopping for a motor driven major appliance such as a washer or refrigerator, this do-it-yourself "stethoscope" is a handy tool to carry. While admittedly more crude than the instrument your doctor listens with, it is surprisingly effective in helping to pinpoint the location of any unusual motor noises. Noisy appliance motors tend to forecast future repair problems, and unless you are handy with tools and have time as well as inclination to overhaul the motor, a fairly expensive repair bill can result.

The homemade appliance "stethoscope" requires only a screwdriver. To use, push the metal blade against the appliance body at the point where noise seems to originate while at the same time pressing the handle firmly against the lower portion of your ear. Noises and vibrations are magnified in much the same way as when we try to listen through a door using a drinking glass as an amplifier. Any severe grinding noises are likely indicators of a problem bearing, which is relatively expensive to replace if you do not have the time, patience, ability, and tools to make the change yourself.

*Thermometers.* The easiest of all measurements is that of temperature. Bring an accurate thermometer of the proper type and range to check the temperature of freezers and refrigerators at several different shelf levels when shopping for these appliances. Rather than asking the seller whether a freezer registers true zero, check for yourself using a freezer thermometer. This is a useful gauge to keep in the freezer after purchase so that you can note any temperature variations due to an increase in the ambient temperature during summer weather or during a peak period of food freezing.

Temperature is critical in many appliances. A refrigerator and freezer both depend on close control of this factor for the maintenance of quality and length of life for the food in storage. A difference of 10 degrees within a freezer cuts potential storage time in half! When looking for a kitchen range, check the oven temperature after the initial preheating period. In a well designed range, a moderate temperature should be reached after preheating 10 minutes or less. Sometimes range calibration service is offered without charge to the customer by a local utility. Under these circumstances, perhaps temperature accuracy may be a less important factor in your selection when other choices need to be weighed. However, the maintenance of correct temperature after calibration adjustments are made is still critical.

Though difficult to check before purchase, the accuracy of thermostatic controls found on portable frypans and saucepans can be determined with an immersion thermometer. A quick check without using any equipment at all can be made by boiling water in the pan using a higher temperature setting for speed, then turning the temperature control to 212°F. to determine whether or not the boiling level can be maintained. When checking the thermostatic accuracy at higher temperatures, use oil and a deep fat thermometer, comparing the results with that level indicated on the control dial. However, many appliances have been calibrated so that the correct temperature of food is maintained when cooking with the cover on since this generally is the preferred method of preparation. When heating without a cover, we found that the temperature generally ranges 15° to 25°F. below that recorded when the cover is in place. This is somewhat dependent upon the shape and size of the pan and the fit of the cover.

### Additional Test Equipment

Although not in the general context of simple test equipment to take with you when checking appliances before purchase, two instruments are highly valuable for electrical trouble shooting. Both would be valuable additions to the stock of tools in your home.

*Neon test lamp.* The less expensive of the two, this test lamp can be purchased for under a dollar in hardware stores. Use it to determine whether electric circuits in the home wiring system or within a single appliance are carrying power. Another use is that of checking for proper grounding of convenience outlets and relative safety of grounding adapter devices. Using these three-pronged adapters in preference to properly installed grounded wall receptacles is not recommended. However, since they do commonly exist, a test for grounding performance is preferable to accepting their work on simple faith.

GROUNDING ADAPTER TEST

1. Attach the adapter pigtail to a paint-free section of the receptacle plate screw.

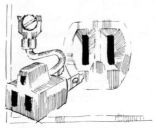

2. Insert lead A of the test lamp into the ground opening and lead B into one of the two remaining slots as shown. IMPORTANT: hold the insulated part of the leads as you are now dealing with live circuits and greater care is necessary than when using only flashlight batteries.

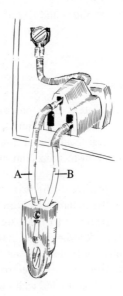

3. Repeat the test, moving lead B to the second slot, leaving A in the same position.
4. The neon bulb should glow in one of the two positions if a proper ground is present.

Should this not occur, make one further check, inserting lead A into one slot and lead B into the other as shown. The light should glow in this position if the outlet is energized. It is important to realize that these adapters are not considered a safe form of grounding because of the many variables present in their installation. Rewiring is the only sure method.

*Volt-ohm meter.* Though a more expensive instrument, a suitable meter still can be found for under $15 that will be satisfactory for the vast majority of appliance testing. Use this device to check for continuity and grounds with greater sensitivity than the continuity testlight can give. You also can check for resistance in a control circuit or verify voltage level when you are in doubt about the level of input. Use of this meter assumes some electrical knowledge. The list of references at the end of the book can be helpful in gaining some knowledge of basic principles as well as offering suggestions on the purchase and potential uses for the volt-ohm meter in appliance repair.

# 3

# major appliances

The average cost of the four major appliances found most frequently in American homes — automatic washer, dryer, range, and refrigerator — is approximately $1,000.[1]

With the substitution of several used or surplus appliances for new purchases, this figure can be substantially reduced. The thrift-minded consumer can benefit from the capriciousness of many appliance owners if he is willing to make some compromises on design features and special options.

## REFRIGERATORS

Consumer demand for color, special finishes, frost-free construction, enclosed condenser coils; automatic icemakers and ice dispensers, as

---

[1]"Replacement & Trade-in Sales Survey," *Merchandising Week, Fifty Years of Statistics & History* (February 28, 1972), p. 70. Based on average cost figures: washer $229, dryer $173, range $238, refrigerator $313.

well as greater total capacity, has contributed to the trend of early replacement, prior to actual necessity from a functional point of view. The market saturation level for refrigerators is the highest of all appliances, 99.8 per cent of the wired homes in the U.S.[2]

As a result of this almost total market saturation, refrigerator replacement purchases are high. Many of the surplus refrigerators can serve second families well at a fraction of the cost of a new model.

## Availability and Cost

In 1971 almost half of the new refrigerator purchases for home use involved a trade-in, and while roughly 50 per cent of these were subsequently junked by the dealer, quite a few used models were offered for resale.[3] Many good buys for under $100 can be found at appliance stores that offer these trade-ins for resale. Frequently, such purchases are accompanied by a three-month guarantee on parts and labor. Generally, personal classified newspaper ads offer similar models at a savings of nearly half that charged by an appliance store. However, a guarantee from a private seller is difficult to enforce and should be considered less valuable than that given by an established firm.

Late model refrigerators are more frequently found through private sales sources than through retail outlets. Often family relocation forces the sale of the top-of-the-line, year-old refrigerator at about half the original cost. One advantage of such private sales, not available when dealing with a retail outlet, is the chance to inspect and test the appliance in the present owner's home. The wary buyer can learn much about past use, care, and installation during the initial visit. When any appliance is plugged in and operating, systematic checking can go a long way in pointing out any future problems the buyer is likely to encounter.

Schools may be eligible to buy ranges and refrigerators on a manufacturer's purchase plan calling for periodic trade-ins. The used appliances are subsequently resold by the dealer, school district, or in some instances, the local utility. While these vary in quality and condition, they usually are better than average values, often carrying a new parts and service warranty. Expect a minimum of a 20 per cent discount when buying such an appliance.

[2]"Saturation Index for Key Products," *Merchandising Week, Fifty Years of Statistics & History* (February 28, 1972), p. 66.
[3]"Replacement & Trade-in Sales Survey," p. 66.

Nearly 40 per cent of the annual home refrigerator sales in the United States take place between the months of June and September.[4] This is due partly to the introduction of new models during this period and partly because of a consumer desire for automatic icemakers which is heightened by the warm weather in much of the country during this period. In addition, a certain number of replacements are made because of refrigeration failure — expedited to a degree because of the increased motor load that a higher ambient temperature imposes. For greater refrigeration selection, check the classified section of your local newspaper during these months as many families offer their older appliances for sale directly rather than trade them in when buying new models. Furthermore, many appliance dealers discourage trade-ins even when the surplus refrigerator is in excellent working condition.

While surplus freight damaged appliances may arrive in the marketplace at any time, the summer months, when more deliveries occur, are the best times to search for these buys.

Newspaper ads often mention damaged merchandise at bargain prices. Another source to check is the classified telephone section. Look under "Liquidators" and "Salvage Dealers," and also check the outlets advertising under "Electric Appliances" for special ads indicating the sale of freight damaged equipment. The retail store outlets for mail order firms are other good sources to check when looking for this type of surplus equipment.

### Service Life Expectancy

Not only is the 16-year life expectancy for refrigerators one of the longest of the major appliance group, but the total repair bill tends to be one of the smallest as well. A survey of necessary repair costs for refrigerators up to eight years old showed an average expense of $15. This repair figure tended to be considerably lower than that required for other major appliances. Interestingly enough, most refrigerator repairs reported were due to minor breakage of plastic parts, clogging of defrost drains, gasket failure and inaccurate calibration of temperature control settings. Nearly one-third of the repairs arose because of the non-durability of parts.[5]

---

[4]"Retail Sales Patterns by Regions, Seasons, Months," *Merchandising Week, 1972 Statistical & Marketing Report* (February 28, 1972), p. 82.

[5]"Refrigerator Repairs," *Consumer Reports* (January, 1966), p. 26.

While special knowledge is not required to spot these more obvious defects in a secondhand refrigerator, sufficient time is needed to check thoroughly before buying.

Most appliance servicemen seem to agree that the manual defrost refrigerators are the most repair-free of all and the least expensive to operate. However, the potential market for these models shrinks each year and actually very few of these refrigerators are manufactured except in the smaller sizes for special installations.

Before deciding on which model to purchase in terms of features, style, and price, consider the capacity needed for your individual family situation. The average refrigerator purchased today has a capacity of 14 cubic feet, and the consumer trend is toward buying even larger models. Increased refrigeration capacity makes it possible for the homemaker to shop less frequently, thus saving both time and money. As a guide, if a family of two were to shop once a week for fresh food, using a combination refrigerator freezer, a nine cubic foot fresh food section and two cubic foot freezer section would be considered adequate. To this figure, add an extra cubic foot of storage space in both sections for each additional family member. And though these guidelines are generally sound, food preparation habits may alter any suggestions to a great extent.

## General Buying Guidelines

Refrigerators come in a great variety of sizes, models, and types to satisfy individual family needs. Though it is hard to point out features that will suit all these needs, the following construction features are worth considering whether purchasing a new or used refrigerator:

*Door.* Left, right, or interchangeable doors are available for specific needs. Sturdy hinges, tight fitting gasket, and convenient handles are needed.

*Frost removal.* Whether you select a manual defrost, automatic defrost, or frostless model will depend upon your budget and personal inclination. The addition of a fan and heating element necessary for frost-free construction adds to the initial purchase as well as to the subsequent utility cost. Frostless models cost up to twice as much to operate as those forming frost within the inside chamber.

However, convenience of cleaning is certainly another valid consideration.

*Storage capacity.* Consider family needs and purchasing habits as well as kitchen space. If condenser coils discharge heat at the rear of the refrigerator, space must be allowed at the top and sides for air circulation.

*Door shelves.* They should be easy-to-clean, adjustable, and sturdily constructed so that they will last and last. However, when considering these spaces for food storage, remember temperatures are at least several degrees higher here than in the main food chamber.

*Frozen food compartment.* Consider capacity required based on your needs and the existence or absence of a separate freezer in the home. Evaluate ice cube capacity, shelf and door storage in relation to your needs. Ideally, a true freezing compartment will maintain a temperature of $0^0$ F. or below.

*Other storage features.* Adjustable and removable shelves make cleaning easier and facilitate interior adjustments to accommodate tall or bulky food items. Meat keepers, vegetable crispers, and other special storage containers can be handy or a problem depending upon construction and size. Inspect all before purchasing. They should all be easy to clean and rustproof. Be sure drawers and sliding shelves move easily.

*Ease of cleaning.* Rounded corners and seamless liner construction facilitate cleaning. Many newer refrigerators are on rollers which encourage more frequent cleaning behind these bulky appliances. When these are not included with a refrigerator, separate appliance rollers can be added, providing that about two inches of extra clearance space exists. When adding rollers, any rigid plumbing for icemakers will need to be replaced with flexible plastic tubing.

*Temperature control.* Refrigerator-freezer combinations with two separate cold control systems are more satisfactory in maintaining proper food chamber temperatures than those with only one dial.

*Special features.* Select those needed to suit your individual situation: juice can dispenser, heated butter conditioner, sliding or swing-out shelves, frostless construction, top, bottom, or side-by-side freezer location.

**Surplus Appliance Check List**

When shopping for a used refrigerator, it is well to check the following points before making your selection:

*Condition of interior and exterior finishes.* Though a break in the finish can be repaired, the purchase price should reflect your effort. High humidity, normal within the food chamber, increases the rust potential of the base material. Ideally, any refrigerator interior should be smooth with as few crevices as possible to collect soil. When shopping for a used appliance, you will need to check further for cracks in the plastic liner. These occur all too frequently.

*General cleanliness.* A less than clean interior is a problem that should not be ignored when buying a secondhand refrigerator. Chlorine bleach, activated charcoal, baking soda, and detergent can help to freshen the food chamber but prevention of the problem is always the preferable method. Sniff carefully before you buy! Most furniture and equipment responds well to a pail of soapy water and a liberal dose of elbow grease, but refrigerators left stored, unused with doors closed for long periods of time, often accumulate odors difficult to remove. In instances where spoiled food has remained within the chamber for an extended period of time, deodorizing the interior is an almost impossible task. Avoid such purchases.

*Door gasket.* Ideally, the rubber or plastic gasket mounted to the refrigerator door should fit so snugly that a piece of paper the thickness of a dollar bill can be pulled between the closed door and the adjacent surface only with difficulty. Admittedly, this is a somewhat stringent test but you might try it at several points on the refrigerator door. When warm air leaks into a refrigerator, your utility expense rises sharply, and maintaining proper temperature within the food storage section becomes almost impossible. If the gasket is old and ineffective but the refrigerator an otherwise good buy, consider replacing the strip yourself. Chapter Seven tells how. Most replacements will only cost about $5 and take only 15 minutes. In some cases an adjustment can be made in the door latch to compensate for a worn gasket. Often the screw channels are movable to allow for a closer fit.

*Condenser coils.* These coils facilitate the exchange of heat from the inside food chamber to the surrounding area outside the refrigerator.

When the coils are insulated with a heavy layer of dust, heat exchange is difficult and the motor must work harder to cool the interior cavity, thus shortening the life expectancy of the appliance. While impossible to rule out any seller's tendency to clean an appliance thoroughly just before advertising for sale, this does not always seem to be the case. Often, a check for cleanliness gives an indication of former care. Most commonly, the condenser coils are located at the upper back of older refrigerators. In newer models, coils can be found at the bottom front of the appliance under a protective grill. Others may be completely enclosed with a fan for heat exchange.

*Freezing compartment door.* Look for well adjusted hinges with "spring" remaining. When hinges sag, adequate cooling within the freezer section is practically impossible. Sprung hinges are common in older refrigerator evaporator sections when owners have provided little care and maintenance.

*Freezing compartment temperature.* Check the interior temperature with a refrigerator-freezer thermometer. An evaporator-type compartment rarely holds food below $15^{0}$F. and is not a true freezer but should be used only to store frozen food a few weeks or to make ice cubes. A true freezer registers $0^{0}$F. or below. Check the interior temperature at several points, perhaps in the back corners and at the front of the enclosure near the door. The temperature level is not always even throughout the freezing compartment.

*Refrigerator compartment temperature.* Well designed, efficient refrigerators consistently maintain temperatures somewhat below the $40^{0}$F. level necessary for food preservation. Lower temperatures are preferred in some sections of the food chamber to protect food quality. A more ideal storage temperature for milk is $35^{0}$F., for meat $29^{0}-31^{0}$F. if a separate meat drawer or compartment is provided, and for most fruits and vegetables commonly refrigerated, $32^{0}-35^{0}$F.

*Motor noise.* Since domestic refrigerators commonly operate on 120 volt circuits, there is little reason to buy a used refrigerator without first testing it. Listen to the motor when the "on" cycle begins, checking for any unusual noises. Former installation on uneven flooring or a lack of maintenance often forecasts future repair bills.

*Refrigeration cycles.* The "on" cycle of different refrigerators varies in length. In addition to design variables, ambient temperature has an effect on this period and during warm weather the "on" time can be lengthened noticeably. Van Zante found the operating time nearly doubled when the ambient temperature rose from 70°F. to 90°F. in all but the two-door refrigerator-freezers. Even in the two-door models, the "on" cycle increased by over 40 per cent.[6]

Under normal conditions a refrigerator motor should not run more than one-third the total time. When you encounter equipment that runs almost continuously, it is well to check a few common problems first. Some can be corrected with a minimum of effort; however, if long standing, the motor will already have suffered. A refrigerator motor might run continuously if the condenser is unable to exchange heat effectively as in the case of improper installation in a confining niche or when the coils are heavily insulated with dirt. In other instances, the door seal may be defective, the cold control set improperly or perhaps a large quantity of warm food has just been added all at one time. However, in other more serious cases, a partial loss of refrigerant may have occurred, and this is a problem you do not need.

*Evaporator condition.* The evaporator is located in the cooling compartment where ice trays are found. In older models, ridges where coils were imbedded may be visible, but in newer models the walls are of flush construction. When manual defrosting is necessary, check to see that ice removal was not expedited in the past with a knife or sharp tool. If the evaporator coil had been completely punctured by such a practice, the refrigerant would already have escaped and there would be no more cooling action. However, as a precaution against future loss, check for dents, worn areas, or other indications of indifferent maintenance.

## DISHWASHERS    1775533

The addition of an automatic dishwasher to the kitchen can save the homemaker an average of 36 eight-hour work days over a year's

[6]Helen J. Van Zante, *Household Equipment Principles* (Englewood Cliffs, N.J.: Prentice-Hall, 1964), p. 263.

time.[7] While this period varies depending upon family size and food habits, the dishwasher is nevertheless a substantial timesaver, usually cutting kitchen cleanup time in half. The ease with which the sink and kitchen counters can be kept clear of dirty dishes while cooking tends to speed both the meal preparation and cleanup processes. Besides saving time and reducing clutter, an automatic dishwasher lowers the level of bacteria remaining on tableware and reduces the incidence of family colds and other infections.

While a dishwasher can serve many family needs, good serviceable models are not the most readily available appliances found in the surplus market. However, with patience and determination, a good buy can be located.

## Availability and Cost

In most cases, salvage shops and retail appliance stores offer few dishwashers worthy of serious consideration. The vast majority of trade-ins are junked by the dealer and consequently never offered for resale, partly because of high reconditioning costs and a low market value for used dishwashers. Salvage shops frequently carry dishwashers for under $25. Though the condition of most is dubious, some might be worth consideration by the family with a mechanically minded member who enjoys "tinkering," because without a doubt, "tinkering" will be necessary.

A freight damaged dishwasher might be an excellent buy if defects are of such a nature that they can be hidden during installation or if the total savings is sufficient to merit refinishing. However, beware of nicks or cuts in the interior finish; the constant water and detergent action during washing will cause the exposed steel surface to rust very quickly.

The personal classified ad section is the best source available for nearly new, serviceable dishwashers. Some are offered for sale by families moving into newly-built homes where appliances are part of the purchase package. In these cases, you often can find dishwashers offered for sale at 60 per cent of the new price even though they are only a year or two old and still in excellent condition.

[7]Elaine K. Weaver, Clarice E. Bloom, Hajean Feldmiller, "A Study of Hand versus Mechanical Dishwashing Methods," *Ohio Agricultural Experiment Station Research Bulletin 772,* 1956, p. 15.

## Service Life Expectancy

In a study of dishwasher repair costs, the average fee for service among appliances one to eight years old was found to be $20. It must be remembered that this was an average figure, and considerable variation was found among different dishwasher brands.[8] While many of the reported repairs could have been made be a mechanically minded owner, a surprising number of problems could have been averted if proper cleaning and loading procedures had been observed. Use and care manuals for dishwashers are filled with ideas to help ensure good washing results with a minimum of service problems. However, few consumers seem to heed the suggestions. And though many manufacturers advertise that no preparation for washing is needed beyond that of "shaking off the loose pieces of food," considerably less cleaning and maintenance is required when more thorough scraping of plates precedes automatic dishwashing.

Little research is available on dishwasher life expectancy; however, manufacturers and service personnel tend to think in terms of a service range from seven to 15 years. Use, installation, and general maintenance of the dishwasher frequently have as much to do with the appliance lifespan as general construction and materials. The dishwasher is a much misused appliance.

## General Buying Guidelines

While dishwasher needs vary with the individual family situation, the following features are worth considering whether shopping for a new or used appliance:

*Capacity.* This varies from five to 17 table settings. The best capacity is dependent upon family size and the number of dishes and utensils used in meal preparation and service. Remember that oversized glasses, platters, and pots require more space than the standard items.

*Type.* Free standing, built-in, or portable dishwashers are available. Some portable-type models are "convertibles"; these may be permanently installed at a later time if you desire. A convertible can be your best buy when planning to move to a home without a dishwasher at a later time. Installation costs are a factor to consider when deciding on either of the built-in versions. In some instances, these charges have equalled the cost of the appliance itself.

[8]"Dishwasher Repairs," *Consumer Reports* (March, 1967), p. 147.

*Top or bottom loading arrangements.* Top loading dishwashers require less clearance space in front of the machine but demand more bending by the homemaker when loading and unloading. Generally, front loading machines are considered easier to load and unload. However, if economy is the major consideration, they tend to cost more initially.

*Interior tub construction.* The tub liner needs to be resistant to the inherent stains, heat, moisture, and strong detergent solutions. Fiber glass, plastic, or porcelain enamel liners are all common. Each has its good and bad features, but basically all serve fairly well.

*Racks.* For greatest utility, rack arrangements should allow for the most flexible loading possible. Today's dishes, glasses, and pots are not standard in size and shape. We need to consider, too, the placement of small items that tend to fall through the regular rack sections. Racks should be coated with a rust resistant, durable covering that will be able to withstand constant washing action and dish abrasion.

*Appliance cabinet.* The cabinet is usually of baked or porcelain enamel over steel, copper, brushed chrome, or stainless steel. When selecting a dishwasher, consider the care required before purchasing. A wood or vinyl top presents another maintenance dimension but still may be desired for appearance's sake.

*Controls and washing options.* Controls should be easy to use and offer desired flexibility in use. Weigh the number of times you will use "Rinse and Hold," "Utility Wash," or any other settings on the more deluxe dishwashers before purchasing. While it may seem like a marvelous idea to warm your dinner plates on the "Plate Warm" setting, most often the dishwasher will have soiled dishes already loaded from meal preparation at the time warm plates are needed. In addition, to circumvent this problem, any dishwasher that can be manually turned to "Dry" can be used to warm plates.

*Insulation.* Dishwashers are somewhat noisy at best. When models do not have sufficient sound deadening insulation, this can be very annoying.

### Surplus Appliance Check List

When shopping for a used or otherwise surplus dishwasher, it is well to consider the following features before committing oneself:

*Space and installation requirements.* Strange as it may seem, some
consumers still buy dishwashers that do not fit in the allocated
spot. Generally, this problem is more prevalent when buying a
portable model. While some lack of dimension standardization
among manufacturers contributes to this problem, a tape measure
accurately applied can eliminate most of the difficulty. Check
costs of dishwasher installation before buying. Adequate electrical
capacity, hot water, and drainage facilities are necessary for efficient dishwasher operation. If the costs are to be kept to a minimum
when installing a built-in model, all must be near the proposed
location. If this is not the case, or if extensive cabinet and
counter alterations are necessary, a portable dishwasher may be
more feasible in your situation.

*Interior and exterior finishes.* Cracked or chipped enamel exposes the
steel body to detergents, hot water, and steam, all of which speed
rusting action. When considering a secondhand dishwasher, look
carefully for telltale brown stains near the impeller or wash arm,
gasket, and hinges. These are common wear spots and frequently
the first areas of rust.

*Motor noises.* Listen carefully as the dishwasher goes through the
complete cycle. Excessive vibration of the motor shaft forecasts
future repair bills. When installing, be sure the floor is level or
adjustments can be made in the dishwasher base, as this problem
is one of the major causes of vibration damage. Before starting
the dishwasher, turn the washer arm by hand to see if it revolves
smoothly without "play" or wobbliness. The fit should be fairly
snug.

*Door gasket.* Check the condition of the rubber gasket. Resiliency is
needed here to keep water *inside* the dishwasher. Gaskets can be
replaced but your effort should be considered when choosing among
several appliances offered for sale.

*Electrical connections.* When possible, remove the appliance panel and
check the wiring insulation for any breaks or burned areas. Wiring
is visible in some dishwasher models only through the bottom of the
cabinet. In these cases, the dishwasher must be turned on its side
if such a check is to be made. If you think this is too great a problem

at the time of purchase, the situation will not improve when the need for repair arises, whether handled by you or a serviceman. Think twice!

*Pump condition.* While checking the electrical connections, look for water leakage near the pump area or hose connections. This is one of the most common dishwasher repair problems. If leakage has occurred in the past, a telltale water stain usually remains where detergent and minerals from the water supply have dried on the finish. If this is the case, the gaskets are likely to need replacement. While repair is possible, it is a more time consuming job than installing the door gasket. If the motor shows any sign of exposure to water, investigate *very* thoroughly before purchasing, as an appliance motor burns out quickly from contact with water and detergent. The best advice would be to look for another dishwasher.

## FREEZERS

A secondhand freezer is probably one of the best buys in the entire surplus equipment market if the buyer makes a few simple tests and takes time to check the most common points of wear. As with other appliances, it is always well to look for well known brands and models when buying a freezer. With proper care, a surplus freezer can provide years of trouble-free operation and be an excellent buy for many families.

For background information on past performance, you might check the public library file of consumer magazines that publish findings of their test laboratories. However, when weighing such information, remember that design features and performance levels change from year to year. In addition, certain features, perhaps of less importance to you, may have been given considerable weight in the final recommendation.

Before shopping, take time to consider your actual need for a home freezer. Such a purchase can represent a dollar savings to the family budget only when used wisely. A freezer allows a family to take advantage of "specials" when prices are low, preserve surplus foods at the season of abundance, and perhaps ensure better use of leftovers, although this latter point is sometimes suspect. The added cost of packaging materials and electricity needs to be calculated as well. For economical operation, a fairly rapid food turnover at a near capacity freezer load is necessary. We all defeat freezer economy by storing leftovers of dubious quality in large amounts to appease our sense of thrift. Similarly, we are not utilizing a freezer to the best advantage when we stock an abundance of commercially frozen foods that are readily available at the same price throughout the year.

However, even if a freezer does not cut the family food budget, it can offer certain advantages for the working homemaker or facilitate guest meals for the family who likes to entertain on the spur of the moment. (The freezer is also of great benefit to the rural family.) With a freezer in the home, fewer trips to the grocery store will be necessary. The homemaker can prepare food in advance when extra time is available for use at a later time when minutes count.

A greater variety of food is possible even for the small family. As an example, under ordinary conditions of storage, it is difficult for the average family to have a variety of sandwich breads on hand. A freezer makes it possible to stock a number of kinds, thawing only a few slices at a time when desired. If you prepare daily sack lunches, save time by making a week's supply of sandwiches all at the same time and then freezing them. Each morning your family can pick up a sandwich, piece of fruit and whatever else is designated for the day with a minimum of fuss, freeing you during the busy breakfast period. The sandwiches will thaw before lunchtime.

Freezer placement is important from a mechanical as well as a functional standpoint. The ideal location is in a dry, well ventilated, cool area away from heating appliances such as the range or dryer. If a choice exists, avoid strong sunlight as well. When the ambient temperature is high, a freezer motor runs for longer periods of time in order to maintain the internal freezing level. Generally, any enclosed placement such as a niche should be avoided because of the restricted air circulation, but check installation directions for specific requirements. Home freezers are most conveniently located near the food preparation work center. Unfortunately, many kitchens lack sufficient space for an extra appliance of this size and the family freezer is then relegated to a garage or basement location. Before deciding upon a freezer purchase, weigh carefully the convenience of your available space. Possibly a combination refrigerator-freezer would be a better choice where kitchen space is at a premium.

While capacity estimates are difficult when individual family needs are concerned, an allowance of six cubic feet of freezer space for each family member may serve as a purchasing guideline. However, the access to home grown produce, bulk meat purchasing options, and meal management habits in general may alter this "average" capacity requirement to a great extent. Capacities, often quoted in "pounds," may be somewhat misleading to the ordinary consumer and should not be taken literally. As we all know, a pound of bread is considerably different in size from a pound of hamburger.

### Availability and Cost

Only 26 per cent of the new freezer sales were accompanied by a trade-in appliance; however, of these only one third were junked by the dealer. Many taken in trade were offered for resale. Over 40 per cent of the new freezer sales took place during the period between June and September.[9] This is an excellent time to check the personal newspaper ads for used freezers that become surplus after the purchase of a new model.

If you can forego the current model and be somewhat flexible about a choice of color, a savings of roughly half the new freezer price can be realized when purchasing a two- to five-year-old model. Older freezers with much service remaining can be located through classified newspaper ads for under $75. The cost of a similar used freezer when purchased from an appliance store is just about double that charged by a private seller. However, reconditioning costs and the value of a dealer guarantee need to be weighed before making your decision.

Chest freezers with comparable capacity carry lower price tags than upright models and, if sufficient floor space is available, may suit a family's needs just as well. Since heat rises, chest freezers actually lose less cold than upright models each time the door is opened — costing proportionately less in operational expense. Because of this factor, they tend to have a more even distribution of cold throughout the entire storage cavity than that found in upright models. On the other hand, the greater convenience in loading and unloading most upright freezers should not be discounted when making your selection.

### Service Life Expectancy

The 15-year life expectancy of a new freezer can be lengthened

[9] Replacement & Trade-in Sales Survey," pp. 71-72.

considerably with proper maintenance and correct installation. While an estimate at best, the especially long average life span of 11 years predicted for the used freezer may make such a purchase very attractive to many families. While the cooling mechanism in freezers is very similar to that found in refrigerators, fewer repairs to interior parts would be necessary because of the relatively simple interior chamber construction with less compartments that show wear and tear at an early date. Previous use, care, and installation determine to a great extent the future life of this appliance.

**General Buying Guidelines**

Whether selecting a freezer from either the new or used market, consider the following appliance features before purchasing:

*Storage capacity.* Freezers vary in size ranging from three to 26 cubic feet of storage space. Your needs are dependent upon family size, access to home grown food, and meal management habits.

*Freezer types.* Whether you select the upright or chest-type freezer depends upon available space and clearance, budget, flooring, and desire for loading convenience.

*Ease of cleaning.* Smooth interior and exterior surfaces with a minimum of crevices and unnecessary trim speed cleaning. Freezers can be purchased with manual or automatic defrost features as well as the frostless option.

*Temperature control.* A temperature of at least $0^0$F. is desirable in the frozen food storage areas. A separate compartment for fast freezing where temperatures are below this maintenance level is highly desirable.

*Doors.* The door construction is an important consideration in freezer selection. A good gasket is necessary to maintain desirable temperature level. Sturdy hinges are required for both types but a chest freezer needs counterbalanced hinges for safety.

*Special features.* Select those really necessary for your family situation; then consider the features that would be "desirable" if your budget allows. A few that might merit your consideration are: a warning signal indicating a temperature rise or power failure, built-in lock, pull-out racks, trays or baskets for easy food storage.

*Thoughts about freezer food plans.* A few have merit — very few. Before signing, compare the cost of freezers without the food plan and then compare the cost of the food alone. Your findings will eliminate many freezer food plans before going one step further. Next, investigate the general food quality, the grade and cut of meat, the variety and required minimum size of the order. Consider too, the extras such as delivery, carrying charges, food substitutions and the length of time a contract remains in force plus any cancellation charges. Generally, freezer food plans do not satisfy family needs and wants, and on the whole they are not an economical method of managing food costs.

**Surplus Appliance Check List**

When considering a secondhand freezer check the following points before buying:

*Interior food chamber.* The liner should be in sound condition, free of cracks or chips, and easy to clean. When spoiled food has remained in a warm freezer for an extended period of time, the resulting odor may be very difficult or impossible to remove. To clean a freezer, wash with a solution of two tablespoons baking soda and one quart warm water. If excessively soiled, you may prefer detergent and water as a first step. Should any odor remain, unplug the freezer and leave the door open for several days. Going one step further, activated charcoal when placed in the food compartment of an open freezer sometimes sweetens the most neglected appliance in two or three days. Oftentimes, a fan can speed the action by moving the air more rapidly. Obviously, when buying a secondhand freezer, it is better to avoid the odor problem entirely.

*Exterior shell condition.* Each buyer needs to decide the number of scratches he can tolerate on the exterior finish. Appliance paint is available for making touch-ups to improve the appearance and to seal rust-prone surfaces but the fewer the scratches the better.

*Insulation.* Effective insulation is a must but adequacy is difficult to ascertain when selecting most used freezers. Probably the best way to check effectiveness of the insulation layer is to measure the interior temperature at different locations with a thermometer so that any warmer areas can be detected. In older models, it was possible for freezer insulation to settle, creating certain "hot spots." However, newer foam insulations that are formed in place through chemical action have tended to eliminate this problem to a great degree.

*Chest freezer lid.* Chest freezers need a counterbalanced lid for safety as well as ease in opening. The basic construction of a chest freezer with its depth and horizontal cover makes it a prime safety hazard when young children are present. The possibility of a door snapping shut on a young child is always a consideration and possibly a lock would be worth considering.

*Quick-freeze compartment.* A lower freezer temperature helps to maintain the quality of stored food. Slow initial freezing causes the formation of larger ice crystals which rupture the cell walls of food, releasing juices, and in turn create a mushy texture. A separate quick-freeze compartment or shelf where the temperature is well below the $0^\circ$F. required for maintenance of frozen food is a worthwhile addition to any freezer. Temperatures ranging from $-10^\circ$F. to $-30^\circ$F. are usual within these compartments and the lower the better if food frozen is to retain optimum quality in terms of texture, flavor, and color.

*Food chamber temperature.* True zero and be sure to check it. As shown in Table 3–1, a rise of only $10^\circ$F. cuts in half the safe freezer storage period for most foods. Such a rise in temperature can be a costly problem, and poor temperature control is not an uncommon defect in secondhand freezers. When shopping, remember that if the freezer cold control must be set at the coldest point to maintain $0^\circ$F., a few questions are in order. Even greater demand upon the refrigeration system will be required on a hot humid day to maintain this level of cold.

*Door gasket.* The gasket should be resilient, providing a tight enough seal to keep the cold air in and the warm air out. When checking gasket condition, follow the suggestions discussed under "Refrigerators." The same firm seal is desirable, but since the temperature gradient is even greater in the case of a freezer, good construction becomes more important.

TABLE 3–1

*Recommended freezer storage periods based on temperature variables*

| Food | Storage Period (Months) | | |
|------|------|------|------|
| | *0°F.* | *5°F.* | *10°F.* |
| Beef | 12–15 | 10–12 | 6–8 |
| Poultry | 8–10 | 6– 8 | 3–4 |
| Butter | 6– 8 | 4– 6 | 2–3 |
| Lean fish | 4– 6 | 3– 4 | 1–2 |
| Organ meats | 2– 4 | 2– 3 | 1–2 |
| Ground meat | 4– 6 | 3– 4 | 1–2 |
| Fruit juices | 12–15 | 10–12 | 6–8 |
| Fruits | 10–12 | 8–10 | 3–6 |

*Condenser coils.* They should be clean and clear of obstructions so that exchange of heat is facilitated. These may be located at the upper back of some freezers or at the bottom front behind a protective grill in other models. In most cases, condensers require cleaning several times a year. Vacuum cleaner attachments make the cleaning task easier but be sure to first disconnect the freezer from the electrical outlet. It is poor safety practice to use two electric appliances or wiring devices, both plugged in, at the same time.

*Electric cord connection.* Cord insulation should be sound or it must be repaired before using. If the plug needs repair, check Chapter Seven for directions. Firm connections at the appliance terminals are important too.

*Missing shelves and other parts.* While these may be available from the manufacturer or your local parts distributor, a visit to the salvage outlets or junkyards in your area may save you money. They often carry shelves or other interior parts for refrigerators and freezers. Ice cube trays, while readily available at most hardware and discount stores, are sold here at unbelievably low prices.

## WATER HEATERS

This is one piece of equipment we cannot recommend buying second-hand. While less than 20 per cent of new water heater sales involved a trade-in, very few of these were eventually offered for resale.[10] Almost all are junked by the appliance dealer rather than rebuilt because of the repair costs and subsequent low resale value. While the average cost of a new water heater is relatively low compared with other appliances, additional installation charges can be sizable. It is wise to check several sources before purchasing. If you intend to make the hookup yourself, investigate your local plumbing and utility codes to see what the requirements are.

When buying a water heater, compare prices at several stores before being swayed by a trade-in allowance. Since the actual value of a used heater is almost nonexistent, trade allowances are somewhat suspect. However, it is convenient when you can convince the dealer to remove your old heater at the same time he delivers the new equipment without additional cost.

### Availability and Cost

While used water heaters are not recommended, some good buys can be found in freight damaged surplus heaters sold by reputable dealers. If a new appliance guarantee accompanies the sale and damage is limited to the exterior finish and not excessive for your particular needs, you may wish to benefit from the savings offered. A 25 per cent discount is common.

As an alternate to purchase, water heaters may be rented on a monthly basis in many cities. Sometimes a rental-purchase plan in which payments may be applied to the future purchase can be found. However, check terms and prices of comparable new equipment first, considering installation and depreciation costs as well as the original cost. When investigating a rental-purchase plan, secure in writing the exact terms under which your payments will apply to eventual purchase. Often there is a time factor involved. In addition to rental-purchase arrangements, some utilities offer maintenance-free rental plans at fairly low cost.

### Service Life Expectancy

A water heater is often the first piece of major equipment to fail in the

---

[10] "Replacement & Trade-in Sales Survey," p. 70.

average home. While standard life expectancy figures are unavailable, an estimate of 10 years is common in the trade.

Whether renting or buying a water heater, your operating costs will be lowered if you do not waste hot water. A leaking hot water faucet not only adds to your water and utility bill but the heater must work harder than necessary to make up for this loss, thus shortening its life span to some degree. It is estimated that a very small leak amounting to a loss of 60 drops of hot water per minute wastes 210 gallons of hot water every month. Not only is this a serious waste of water, but such a loss is equivalent (in cost) to adding another person (and his normal water use) to your family. Should you need a further reason for replacing leaky gaskets, check the exact cost with your local utility.

**General Buying Guidelines**

*Capacity required.* Estimate hot water needs first. Consider the needs of your home appliances as well as the 15 to 25 gallons per person per day required for each family member. Not surprisingly, children use more hot water than adults. The tank size and recovery rate together determine the amount of hot water available at any given time. Less storage capacity is necessary when the water heater has a fast recovery rate; however, it should hold what will be needed at one time.

As a general guide to water needs, the following averages might be considered in your heater selection. However, appliance needs, like personal needs, vary considerably.

> Automatic dishwasher: 10 – 14 gallons
> Automatic clothes washer: 10 – 35 gallons per load
> Shower: 5 – 15 gallons, depending on how long you take and
> how hot you like your water
> Tub bath: 7 – 8 gallons
> Non-automatic washers: 12 gallons

*Temperature controls.* They should be easy to read and adjust. Automatic dishwashers require water from 140°F. to 160°F. at the appliance outlet for satisfactory performance. Install the heater as near as possible to avoid heat loss. Every 25 feet of water pipe wastes the heat paid for in one gallon of water every time you turn on the hot water faucet. We often compensate for longer water pipes by turning the thermostat up, but higher temperatures encourage premature heater breakdowns.

*Tank.* Select size and shape to fit your location. If the tank is galvanized or porcelainized, ask for a magnesium rod insertion to prevent corrosion. The chemical properties of your local water supply affect tanks in different ways and it is best to check your local utility for suggestions.

*Insulation.* Rock wool or fiber glass, one to three inches in thickness, will provide necessary insulation.

*Safety valves.* These are necessary to prevent excessive water pressure and protect against dangerously high water temperatures.

*Warranty.* Water heater warranties have had certain ambiguities in the past, especially those sold with a declining scale of dealer responsibility depending upon heater age. Read thoroughly before buying.

## RANGES

Many changes have taken place in range designs during the past few years. In 1972 self-cleaning models were expected to account for 50 per cent of the new electric range sales.[11] If you can forego this feature, better than average bargains are available in the surplus market. While fewer used models with the self-cleaning feature are available through retail or salvage outlets at the present time, more are offered for sale by private parties through the newspaper classified ads. When a family buys a new home complete with built-in appliances, it frequently offers its older equipment for sale. Many nearly new ranges are sold in this manner at a generous discount. Personal and financial problems or changes of residence are more often responsible for sales of relatively new ranges than appliance trade-ins.

The newer electronic and smooth-topped glass ceramic ranges appear occasionally in newspaper ads but with considerably less frequency than the 10-year-old conventional appliance. However, in several years the frequency will probably increase. As consumer choices expand in the new appliance market, a similar increase takes place in the surplus field.

[11]"Ranges 1972,"*Appliance* (February, 1972), p. 55.

## Availability and Cost

Prices of used and surplus models vary from $15 for models with do-it-yourself repair arrangements to $50 off the original price for an unused appliance, often advertised as "still in the original crate." As a precaution, check the accuracy of the "original" price as some are inflated before the "markdown." Fairly new ranges, in the two- to five-year-old category, are frequently offered in the newspaper classified ads for about half the regular new retail price. Many serviceable models, eight or so years old, commonly sell in the $50 to $75 range. Freight damaged ranges may appear in almost any retail outlet from time to time. Special discount-type sales outlets can be found by checking the telephone listings as mentioned previously. In addition, the newspaper classified ads sometimes offer freight damaged ranges.

Secondhand ranges are sold through a variety of outlets. Personal classified ads are the best sources of the nearly new range models. The reputable appliance store that thoroughly reconditions trade-in equipment, offering a 90-day or longer guarantee on parts and labor, is probably the safest source when searching for an older model range. While prices for these ranges generally will be lower when sold by a family, the dealer's guarantee is of greater value to the consumer than a private seller's promise.

Appliance dealers, school districts, and utilities sometimes sell school plan ranges used in home economics classrooms to the general public. A mixed lot as far as quality is concerned, these ranges need to be judged individually. Some carry low price tags and are in excellent condition; others have a worn look and are priced higher than the original school price. Generally, utilities offer school plan ranges at a 20 per cent or greater reduction after they have been used a year or two in the classroom. In some instances, utilities limit such resale to their own employees but it doesn't hurt to ask. Before purchasing any school plan appliance, check the current retail price of similar models so that you have a basis for comparison.

Often, salvage outlets sell 10- to 15-year-old ranges for $50. While low in cost, these purchases do carry some risks. Check thoroughly before bringing any range home from a salvage store. The typical range found in these outlets is a fairly obsolete model, already showing signs of wear. However, if the wiring and switches are in serviceable condition, such a purchase can offer a family several years of operation

at a very low price indeed. However, it does help if you are handy
with tools and know how to replace a heating element.


## Service Life Expectancy

The average life expectancy for a new gas or electric range is 16 years.
The more complex models with rotisseries or programmed oven controls tend to require more repairs than the stripped down models
which initially were more economically priced as well. Whether searching for a new or used range, it is well to select one with only those
features useful in your family situation. Many range accessories go
unused for months or years at a time. Some are never used. All cost
the consumer money that might bring greater satisfaction if spent
elsewhere.


## General Buying Guidelines

There is great diversity in both gas and electric ranges offered for sale.
When shopping for either a new or used range, consider the following
features before buying:

*Range types.* Both gas and electric ranges can be found as free standing,
   slide-in or drop-in models. Built-in surface units and separate ovens
   are also available. Pick the model that suits your kitchen needs.

*Capacity required.* Your meal preparation habits and family size
   determine whether you need two ovens, four or six elements or
   burners, a separate griddle, or any one of the countless range options
   offered in the market. These vary in size from the compact apartment models to the double-oven 40-inch range.

*Controls.* They should be easy to read, grasp, and, as an added plus, be
   removable for easy cleaning. Consider range location for convenient
   and safe use. Reaching across a hot pot can bring a nasty steam burn
   when these controls are located without proper thought about
   safety.

*Exterior surfaces.* Cleanups are easier when a range has as few sharp
   corners and crevices as possible. A cooking top with a slight
   depression to catch spillovers before they run down the side of the
   range also saves effort. Ranges are commonly finished in porcelain

enamel; however, stainless steel, brushed chrome, or copper are also available.

*Oven construction.* A number of features are important in a well designed oven. The oven should be vented through an opening that will not soil adjacent wall surfaces. Often this opening is at the base of a cooking unit. Look for rust resistant racks with a lock stop for safety. Four or five shelf supports are desirable to vary utensil placement. Adequate insulation is required to keep the heat inside. And last but not least, an oven should be as easy to clean as possible. Removable oven liners or doors help speed the job and a self-cleaning range might be considered the ultimate in convenience.

*Oven temperatures.* Earlier ovens did not have a great selection at the lower temperature range. If you roast or bake at low temperatures, warm plates, or use the oven to keep food warm, look for controls beginning at $140^\circ$F. to $150^\circ$F.

*Broiler.* If located in a separate compartment, many of the same suggestions mentioned under "oven construction" apply here as well. In addition, an easy-to-clean broiler pan with slits or holes to drain drippings is a necessity.

*Surface units or burners.* The easier to disassemble for cleaning the better. Consider the number of large and small units or burners required. Weigh the need for a high speed or temperature controlled range-top feature.

*Automatic ignition.* Automatic ignition for top, oven, and broiler burners on gas ranges adds convenience and safety.

*Special features.* Consider those necessary for your family situation. While a number of options are offered, those listed are more commonly requested: meat thermometer, timed oven controls and appliance outlets, thermostatically controlled surface unit or burner, high speed surface unit, self-cleaning feature, glass oven door, rotisserie, griddle.

*A word about automatic oven controls.* Considerable variety exists in the design of automatic meat probes and programmed oven systems. These meat thermometers may indicate temperature, buzz a warning signal when selected internal temperature has been reached, turn off the oven, or lower the temperature to a keep-warm setting. Investigate the action of the specific meat probe before buying a range to avoid disappointment. Programmed oven systems may operate on the principle of immediate baking followed by a lower heat keep-warm setting until manually turned off; other models offer a delayed bake feature. The quality of food cooked in both systems varies with the selection of food. What is good for a baked potato is poison for the perishable casserole.

### Surplus Appliance Check List

When looking for a surplus range, the following points may be of help in evaluating the quality and checking possible points of wear:

*Interior surfaces.*  Inspect porcelain oven liners and broiler compart-
ments for chips or crazing of the enamel surface. If the enamel is broken and not resealed, the steel body will rust. Heat and moist conditions found in an oven speed up normal oxidation. Next, check all common areas of wear. Inspect the oven liner flange area near the door for surface damage or dents. Look at hinge connection; check finish near drawers and surface units or burners as well.

*Exterior surfaces.*  Range cabinets are manufactured using a variety of materials and finishes: stainless steel, chrome, glass, glass ceramic, porcelain enamel, synthetic plastic resin-based enamel, iron, steel, and even copper. Commonly used abrasive cleaners dull a porcelain finish. Sometimes appliance wax can restore the luster to some degree. Cleaning and maintaining such a variety of materials takes some thought. Chapter Seven offers general maintenance guidelines that may be of help in specific situations.

Construction is important too. The fewer sharp corners and crevices to collect dirt the better. Cleanliness of exterior and interior range surfaces is highly desirable, although all too rarely found in secondhand ranges.

*Oven doors.*  A well fitting oven door with a good gasket is vital to successful baking. Check for snug fit at the top of the oven door by pulling a piece of paper through in the same manner as suggested in the "Refrigerators" section. While a close fit is desired between the top of the oven door and the liner flange, about 1/8 inch of space is usually present at the bottom edge of the door. In some cases the oven door hinge adjustment can be changed to correct a problem; in others, a serviceman may be required. Check the squareness and fit of the oven and broiler doors before purchasing any range. The tendency to rest heavy pans on the door invites both warping and sprung hinges.

Glass windows in oven doors are popular since the cook can peek at a cake without disturbing the baking process. When buying a secondhand range, if the glass appears cloudy or stained, check to see whether it can be removed for cleaning.

*Oven temperature.* A well designed oven should preheat to a moderate temperature within 10 minutes at the most. If you preheat longer, you are wasting money. Lack of oven temperature calibration is a common problem in the surplus range market. It is not unusual to find an oven as much as 100°F. out of calibration. While an adjustment can be made, unless your local utility provides a free range service, you will probably have a repair bill. Some rotary control knobs are designed so that the user can make an adjustment by simply moving an indicator on the underside. Before buying, you might be wise to remove this knob, checking to see if such adjustment is possible.

*General cleanliness.* Appliance servicemen consider the range the most mistreated of all household equipment. All too frequently a kitchen range receives only a quick wipe rather than the thorough cleaning necessary to discourage residual grease build up. Before buying, look under drip pans and in the broiler-oven cavities for difficult-to-remove residue left by a previous owner. Next, remove the range drawer, checking for rust or soil accumulation. These less accessible areas can serve as an indicator for the quality of past care and maintenance. Residue near elements or burners can cause a fire and, in the case of the gas range, heavy soil interferes with actual combustion. When drip pans and supporting rims are removable, the cleaning is much easier. In some cases, the heating units themselves are detachable, simplifying the process even further.

*Meat probe.* Some difficulty exists in checking the accuracy of this probe and other optional features when buying from a retail outlet or even a private party. If a parts and service guarantee accompanies the sale, be sure to check each feature within the applicable period of time. A quick check of the meat probe's accuracy can be made by placing the sensing probe in a container of hot water along with another thermometer so that you can compare the indicated temperature on the panel dial with that on the test thermometer.

*Timed appliance outlets.* These can be inoperative even though the rest of the range works perfectly. The cost of repair may be as high as $20 so it is well to be advised at the time of purchase. Before rejecting an otherwise good range or calling a repairman, check the 120 volt fuse in the range. Generally, it can be found under one of the surface elements behind a protective shield, in the bottom drawer or, less conveniently, at the back of the range. Missing, loose, or blown fuses are the most common reasons for failure. If this is not the problem and a timer clock is present, check to see if the control is set on "timed." If so, reset to "manual" and your problems may be over.

If you really want to check timer accuracy, connect a small appliance or light to the outlet, setting the clock control ten minutes or so ahead, comparing results.

*Rotisserie.* Engage spit and listen to the motor. A grinding noise forecasts some future repair work. At the same time you might evaluate the motor in relation to your personal level of noise tolerance, remembering that the rotisserie often runs two or three hours at a time while cooking a roast. Many motors, even when in good condition, are so noisy that the rotisserie is seldom used.

## Special Electric Range Considerations

*Electrical connections.* An electric range requires a 240 volt special purpose outlet. If none is present in your home or a new range location is desired, consider the cost of rewiring. The addition of a range circuit is not inexpensive. Some older homes have range outlets designed for permanent hookup rather than the plug-in type of connection. Such installations are really more safely handled by a competent serviceman than a handy husband. However, in these infrequent situations, it might be well to investigate modernizing the electrical outlet itself so that range repairs and cleaning will be facilitated in the future.

New appliance cords or "pigtails" for ranges are available at most hardware and discount outlets if replacement is necessary. The individual wires are color coded or otherwise marked to guide in the correct connection at the terminal block. However, some electrical knowledge is presumed and certain safety precautions are necessary. Several of the references listed at the end of this book can offer advice in this instance.

*Surface, oven, and broiler elements.* When possible, inspect the terminal connections of all heating elements. Wires should have sound insulation without any breaks and the connections should be secure. For safety and longer appliance life, avoid any surplus ranges where insulation is cracked or cut, exposing current-carrying wires, unless you have the necessary knowledge to make needed repairs or plan to have the range serviced before using.

### Gas Range Considerations

*Gas burners.* Most burners can be easily dismantled and cleaned. This construction is a decided advantage when purchasing most second-hand models. However, when any range is very dirty, the selling price should reflect your labor. Pilot valves and ignition tubes that can be dismantled and washed in a strong detergent solution will likewise speed your cleanup.

*Gas burner adjustments.* When a burner is properly adjusted, the flame will be clear blue. When considering a secondhand gas range, turn on the oven and surface burners at the same time, checking to see if the flame from the surface burner tends to "float". While improper air adjustment may be the cause, this floating action also can indicate heat leakage from the oven and thus inadequate insulation. If this is the case, check thoroughly before buying.

In some areas, the local gas utility will make range burner and pilot adjustments on a complimentary basis. If this is not the case and you wish to correct the problem yourself, check the availability of a service manual from the manufacturer or the local utility.

## AUTOMATIC WASHERS

Most automatic clothes washers rely on a series of solenoids operated by timers to control the various laundry cycles and to select water temperature and agitation speed. Depending upon the number of options, the control mechanism can be quite complex. Buying a washer without a written guarantee covering parts and labor is unwise unless you use-test the appliance, observing closely through all the cycles. While it is always a good idea to ask for a guarantee, bear in mind that enforcing the agreement will be difficult, if not impossible, when dealing with a private party rather than a recognized business outlet. It is possible, though, that your request for a guarantee may encourage the seller to be somewhat more factual when discussing appliance condition. Your effort may not be totally in vain.

All automatic washers are constructed with a tub mounted on springs housed inside the body of the machine. The springs, although differing in design, should effectively absorb the extreme vibration that often develops during spin cycles as a result of unbalanced loads or certain other variables. However, even the best spring action cannot compensate for poor installation on an uneven surface. When shopping for a secondhand washer, check the condition of these springs by firmly rocking the tub in all directions. The tub should be freely suspended, not bumping the washer frame at any time.

When moving a washer from one location to another, special care must be taken to protect this spring action. Originally, braces were supplied to hold the inner tub in position during shipping but these are removed before use and most frequently discarded by the first owner. Therefore, when the washer is moved without these braces attached, it should be kept in a near vertical position. Never lay an automatic washer on its side as the supporting springs and guides can slip out of position and may cause damage to the internal wiring. In addition, loading and unloading should be as gentle as possible, and, considering the bulkiness and weight of an automatic washer, this is asking quite a bit.

## Availability and Cost

Serviceable used automatic washers can be found in a variety of outlets. To begin your search, check the newspaper classified advertising section. While most appliance columns have many washer offers, the age varies widely, from ancient to the nearly new. Many appliance and department stores take older models in trade. While the majority of trade-ins are junked, appliance stores tend to recondition and offer for resale more of these than other retail outlets. Some washers taken in trade by retailers requiring more than a simple cleanup are sold to independent appliance repairmen who recondition them before selling. Reputable appliance repair shops can be excellent sources to check for dependable surplus laundry equipment.

Salvage stores are a less dependable source of supply, and unless you are very lucky or have better than average mechanical ability, you would do better elsewhere. Washers found in these shops tend to have very low resale value and, as you might expect, there is usually a reason.

Freight damaged surplus models often appear both in regular retail outlets and special discount-type stores. Check the classified section of your local telephone directory for dealers specializing in these surplus models. Substantial savings can be realized when new models appear on the market, generally during the early summer. See Chapter 10 for a shopping calendar showing normal sales periods.

Washer resale prices tend to be fairly low. Generally, three-year-old machines are advertised through the newspaper personal classified section for roughly half the new retail price. This price seems somewhat dependent upon the seller's whims and circumstances plus the buyer's ability to bargain. Speaking of bargaining, when you find a washer that meets your needs but the price seems out of line, make a counteroffer, leaving your phone number. Often the seller recognizes that his price is too high and he just might call you back before offering the equipment to the next prospect at a lower price. Older models within the five- to ten-year-old range can be found for from $50 to $75. Some have years of service remaining, but let's be honest: you should definitely expect to make some repairs when purchasing any automatic washer over five years old.

### Service Life Expectancy

The life expectancy of the average new automatic washer has been estimated at 11 years. To a greater degree than with many other appliances, the life of a washer reflects its previous care and installation. Overloading the equipment can shorten its life as can non-level installation, excessive soap, or, in many models, the use of high sudsing detergent. Because of design limitations, the front loading machines are more susceptible to damage from regular sudsing detergents than the top loading models. Washers that have been subjected to freezing temperatures, high humidity, or exposure to the outside elements such as those in a garage or carport are also poor choices from the standpoint of future trouble-free performance.

Generally speaking, the older the washer, the greater the average cost of needed repairs will be. The average automatic washer repair bill tends to increase $5 for every year of appliance age.[12] It also seems that the more features and the greater complexity of the washer mechanism, the greater the chance of a repair bill. Whether you expect to make repairs yourself or hire a serviceman, it is well to consider the accessibility of the motor and other parts. A washer with a removable front panel is infinitely easier to work on than one requiring back or bottom access.

## General Buying Guidelines

When selecting either a new or used automatic washer, consider the following points before buying:

*Washing action.* Top loading washers depend upon agitators for washing action. These may be of several different constructions and move in different ways. Front loading machines have a revolving drum with fins or baffles which aid in tumbling the laundry through the water.

*Capacity.* Be somewhat skeptical when reading a washer's capacity rated in "pounds." Remember that washing 15 pounds of heavy work clothes is a different thing from laundering 15 pounds of sheer curtains. Common sense and the size of the inner tub will be a better guide.

*Inner tub.* The surfaces should be smooth, snag-free, and constructed of a material resistant to abrasion, heat, detergent, and water. Porcelain enamel, fiber glass, and stainless steel are commonly used in this construction.

*Cabinet exterior.* Stain resistant finishes of porcelain or baked enamel are most common. Porcelain enamel is used on the top surface because of its greater resistance to commonly used laundry products. A cabinet with a minimum of fragile trim and crevices will be easier to clean and maintain.

*Controls.* Clearly marked, flexible, easy-to-operate controls make wash operation simple for all family members, thus lightening the homemaker's duties.

[12] "Washing Machine Repairs", *Consumer Reports* (March, 1966), p. 143.

*Doors*. A tight seal and sturdy hinges are a must. Consider the opening direction convenient in your laundry installation when purchasing.

*Service access*. Consider the ease of removing the service panel. Time is money, especially at appliance repair rates.

*Washing cycles*. A great number of water temperature and agitation variables are possible. While the need for washer control options is an individual decision, consider the desirability of "cold-warm-hot" wash and rinse settings and a "regular" or "gentle" agitation speed choice so that a greater variety of fabrics can be laundered successfully.

*Special features*. A great many options are available. To name a few: water level adjustment to allow for special needs, separate wash basket for small loads, automatic soak cycle, suds and water return system to allow re-use of wash water.

## Surplus Appliance Check List

When shopping for a surplus washer, check the following features before making your choice.

*Inner tub condition*. Look for a smooth easy-to-clean interior surface of enamel or stainless steel. Check for rust or chipped porcelain areas, especially around the hinges and agitator. Rust inside a washer can damage many dollars worth of clothing and the situation is very difficult to remedy. Condition of the inner door surface and the area surrounding detergent, bleach, or fabric softener dispensers is also indicative of general care received in the past.

*Agitator*. Remove the agitator post found in top loading washers and check the tub condition. The seller may be surprised at what you find underneath it. Frequently, threads catch at the base of the post binding the agitator. In addition, you may find coins, nuts and bolts, rubber bands, and some even more creative things from little boys' pockets. This is a good maintenance practice to continue once you bring the washer home.

*Cabinet construction and finish*. Look for general cleanliness and condition in the outer washer cabinet. However, remember that the outside finish is much easier to retouch with appliance paint than the tub interior and repairs can often be made quite satisfactorily.

Stains on the cabinet do not impair the appliance service life but they may be a consideration depending upon your proposed location. In many cases, a generous application of appliance cleaning wax with a solvent base will remove discolorations; however, dyes or the residue from certain laundry or stain treatment products mar enamel permanently.

*Electrical connections.* Check the insulation of wires and plug. Broken insulation is always a safety hazard but the nature and general location of a clothes washer magnifies this risk substantially. The washer must be grounded for safety.

*Door gasket.* The condition of the gasket on any washing machine indicates whether the laundry room floor will be flooded or remain dry. Because of the wash action, gasket condition is even more critical in front loading machines. While gaskets can be replaced easily and inexpensively if you do the work yourself, the selling price should compensate you for your efforts.

*Belt condition.* If present, check motor pulley belt for slippage, apparent breaks, or flat spots. In most models, tension is correct when the belt can be depressed about one-half inch midpoint between the pulleys. Replacement of the belt, while not difficult, should be considered in making your selection.

*Hose connections.* Check both the intake and drain hoses for deterioration. While hoses can be replaced easily with no great mechanical skill, some allowance in the selling price should be expected.

## NON-AUTOMATIC WASHERS

Non-automatic washers fall into two classifications: the wringer and the spinner types. In the past few years newly designed portable spinner washers have been introduced. While not a new concept, these washers have attracted consumer interest because of their portability and the resulting freedom from permanent installation that the automatics demand. The new spinner washers are more attractive in design than their earlier counterparts and can be stored out of the way under kitchen or bathroom counters for convenient use. Both wringer and spinner washers have a common simplicity of construction but they differ in the method of expelling water from wet laundry.

For economy in original price, maintenance and water requirements, the wringer- or spinner-type washer ranks ahead of the automatic. But if you are thinking of convenience, that's a different story.

### Availability and Cost

As you might guess, more secondhand wringer- and spinner-type washers can be found in small town appliance or secondhand outlets than in urban areas. Homemakers who profess loyalty to these non-automatic washers tend to keep them until the last drop of possible service is gone, but sometimes the machines outlive their owners.

Occasionally, newspapers carry ads for used wringer washers, which generally are priced between $15 and $45. Salvage outlets offer a few from time to time, and curiously enough, these are usually in better condition than the automatic machines. Wringer washers are less likely to be taken in trade when purchasing automatic laundry equipment from an appliance dealer. Therefore, when it comes time to clean out the basement, some of these washers are donated to salvage outlets when they have been serving only an occasional laundry need and space is at a premium.

### Service Life Expectancy

The average new non-automatic washer may be expected to last 10 years and models purchased secondhand should provide six years of service. However, many seem to go on forever. When searching through rural secondhand stores, you can occasionally find a washer dating back to the early 1900s. One family found such a machine with a solid copper wash tub that was built in 1915. This venerable old washer was in remarkable condition despite its age, with only frayed insulation and a worn wringer roller after its many years of service.

When mechanical problems arise, a wringer washer is somewhat easier to repair than an automatic machine. The switching mechanism is a model of simplicity without complex timing controls but the availability of parts may occasionally prove a problem. While distributors offer the surest source of supply, those seeking true economy when purchasing needed parts should check local salvage yards. As an example, wringer roller replacements are often available for under a dollar.

## General Buying Guidelines

When looking for either a new or secondhand non-automatic washer, consider a few general guidelines:

*Capacity.* A wide range exists all the way from countertop portables to the standard wringer or spinner models. Select the tub capacity suitable for your family needs, laundry area, and hot water supply. A clearly marked water line is helpful when filling any machine and discourages excess water which may flood the working mechanism.

*Tub construction.* Smooth stainless, porcelain finished, or plastic lined wash and spin tubs eliminate snagging of garments. They must be able to stand the rigors of heat, water, agitation, and laundry supplies.

*Spinners.* Consider the speed of spin action. Some portable models spin at 2000 RPM, leaving lightweight garments nearly dry. A drain strainer to collect lint during the spin cycle eliminates many a clogged drain hose.

*Cover.* A hinged cover or, at the very least, a hook on which to hang a separate cover is desirable. A snug fitting gasket keeps the water inside where it belongs.

*Cord holder.* A hook that holds the cord off the floor can eliminate insulation damage should the washer be inadvertently rolled over it.

*Timer.* A timer helps standardize washing periods. However, if none is available, the portable one from your kitchen can do double duty.

## Surplus Appliance Check List

When shopping for a used wringer- or spinner-type washer, check the following points to determine previous care and maintenance:

*Interior tub condition.* Unscrew the agitator post, if present, checking the lower tub condition. When considering a spinner-type machine, remove the basket and check the drainage pump area to get some idea of former maintenance. Look for a smooth, crack-free interior finish showing no signs of rust that would stain laundry.

*Exterior tub surfaces.* The common ailments are chipped enamel, rust, and a general lack of cleanliness. Since non-automatics, with the exception of the modern portable models, are unlikely to be stored in other than a very utilitarian laundry area, appearance is not of prime importance. However, a paint touch-up to discourage rust makes good maintenance sense.

*Wringer safety features.* Check the emergency safety release to see that it immediately loosens wringer pressure. This is vitally important for safety. The pressure release must be within easy reach of the operator from any position at the washer and should respond to even light pressure. Do not buy a wringer washer without this safety feature.

*Wringer roller construction.* Controls for forward and reverse action should be easy to reach and operate. The wringer will adjust more easily to different fabric thicknesses and will break fewer buttons if at least one of the rollers is cushioned.

*Balance.* A poorly balanced washer can tip over when the wringer assembly is swung directly away from the tub. Obviously this is dangerous in any situation, but the problem is more acute when young children are present. Even if your washer is well designed, develop the habit of returning the wringer to its proper position after washing to avoid unplanned collisions. Furthermore, the wringer assembly is an attractive support for small children to swing from and the danger of pulling the machine on top of any child is great.

*Drainboard.* Rough edges or corners can snag more fragile laundry. Check for smooth construction and stain-free finish.

*Motor switch.* For safety reasons a washer with an "on" and "off" switch is preferable to that which requires disconnecting by removing the plug from an outlet. When the switch is turned to "on," no sign of arcing or sparks should occur.

*Tub drains.* Water may be drained from the wash tub either by gravity or motor driven pump. Though the electric pump adds to the overall washer cost and requires greater maintenance, it helps keep the laundry floor dry. Many accidents occur in a laundry room because of wet, slippery floors and the possibility of lethal electric shock is increased if you stand on a wet surface. If the tub empties through a bottom drain, a threaded hose connection is handy so that water can be carried directly into the floor drain.

If the washer drain opening does not have such a threaded construction, you might add one so that a hose can be attached to
lessen water spillage.

*Electrical connections.* Any except the antique washer uses electricity
as well as water. This combination can be highly dangerous
when electrical connections are not all they should be safety-wise.
Check the cord insulation, plug, and appliance terminal
connections. Do not buy any washer with unsound connections
unless you intend to repair the problem areas BEFORE using.
If the washer has not been grounded for safety, check Chapter
Seven for instructions. Grounding is especially important in a
laundry appliance.

*Motor and pump condition.* Check motor and pump housings as well
as any visible wiring for signs of water damage due to overfilling
or leakage. Usually the residue from soap or detergent will
leave a telltale mark. While replacement of worn gaskets to stop a
leak is an inexpensive repair that many owners can handle themselves,
water damage to the motor is a more costly problem.

*Agitator drive.* Whenever possible, run the washing machine before
buying so that you can check the smoothness of agitator action.
If the agitator starts with a jerk, the drive mechanism is probably
worn and will need repair or replacement soon. Seek another washer
unless you enjoy do-it-yourself projects.

## CLOTHES DRYERS

Manufacturers advise that the homemaker can save 300 hours a year
with the purchase of an automatic dryer. In addition to this savings
in time, a dryer has several other advantages. Less family clothing
is needed when laundry no longer must be relegated to a once-weekly
job. Fabrics last longer and look better when sun-fading, smog, insects,
and birds are no longer problems.

Most conventional electric dryers require 240 volt electric service,
and while some are convertible to 120 volts, the changeover takes
some electrical knowledge and resulting drying time will be two to three
times greater. Except in the case of small portable models, operating
a dryer on 120 volts is unsatisfactory. If yours is a new installation,

check utility hookup availability and expense before buying a dryer. Any connection requirements should be considered part of the overall appliance cost.

Most dryers require venting to the outside for efficient and safe operation. While the moisture exhausted varies with the load, a gallon an hour during the drying period is not unusual. Placement of the dryer so that venting requires a minimum length of tubing with as few 90° angle bends as possible should be considered. Venting is easiest, least expensive, and most efficient when the dryer is located next to an outside wall. When installation instructions are missing, check your local utility for suggestions on venting a dryer. The average expense ranges from $10 to $30 depending upon the laundry location and how handy you are.

While few condenser dryers are to be found in the market today, you may find one in a secondhand or salvage store. These appliances require a cold water plumbing connection and drain facilities rather than a vent to the outside. A cold water spray runs during the entire drying operation to condense the moisture held in the warm air leaving the dryer drum. Approximately 24 gallons of cold water are needed for condensation when drying the average load of clothes. Such a dryer should never be operated without the spray of cold water.

### Availability and Cost

Nearly half of all new dryer sales involve a trade-in allowance; however, of those taken in, 50 per cent are junked.[13] Often the best place to look for a reconditioned dryer is in an appliance or hardware store. Independent repairmen who may recondition those taken in trade by retail stores are other good sources.

At times, the local newspaper carries classified ads for freight damaged and previous year models. When available, these are usually excellent buys. Personal ads offer more late model used dryers for sale than conventional retail outlets, partly due to family relocations and the availability of laundry equipment in many builders' homes.

In many cases, a three- to five-year-old dryer can be had for one-third the price of new equipment. Strangely enough, dryers carry very low resale prices yet have fairly long service life expectancies. A contributing factor may be the many changes within the last few years in equip-

---

[13] "Replacement and Trade-in Sales Survey", p. 72.

ment design to accommodate the textile and laundry product changes. Many serviceable dryers are offered for sale by private families for about $50. While these rarely have the latest electronic sensing controls, such devices in reality often prove a mixed blessing for the average homemaker.

### Service Life Expectancy

A new dryer correctly installed and maintained should give an average of 14 years of service. Heating element failure is one of the most common repair problems. The price of an element is low (generally under $5), and for the mechanically minded, the installation is one of the easiest to make.

Though no really binding guarantee accompanies a dryer purchased from a private party, if the machine has been use-tested and the mechanism behind the service panel inspected for the more obvious problems, your chances of a major repair bill during a length of time equivalent to any dealer's guarantee are very small indeed.

### General Buying Guidelines

When looking for a new or secondhand dryer, consider the following features in relation to your family needs:

*Cabinet and drum condition.* Look for smooth, durable finishes that are easy to clean. Porcelain enamel or stainless steel are commonly used inside the drying drum. Most often, baked or porcelain enamel over steel is used on the outside of the appliance cabinet.

*Installation requirements.* Gas dryers may use natural, manufactured, or LP gas as fuel. In addition to a gas hookup, they require 120 volt electrical service to operate the motor and fan assembly and possibly to furnish the ignition spark. Most electric dryers require a 240 volt individual electric circuit; however, some may be connected to a 120 volt source. Outside venting is necessary for most standard sized dryers with the exception of the condenser dryers which require a cold water connection and drain. However, these are rarely available today.

*Controls.* A choice of "low" or "regular" heat provides greater flexibility in laundering. A "no heat" setting may be desired as well.

Timed or automatic moisture sensing-type dryer controls are available. Regardless of the type, all controls should be easy to see and operate.

*Special features.* A number are available to suit individual family needs. Several of the most commonly requested are: "damp dry" setting, foot pedal door opening, signal that warns when drying cycle is finished, "no tumble" setting with a rack for drying stuffed animals, tennis shoes, or similar items that create problems in the conventional drying situation.

### Surplus Appliance Check List

When searching for a surplus dryer, check the following construction and operating features:

*Use-test.* When shopping for a secondhand dryer, carry some damp towels in a plastic bag for use-testing. If any unusual noises occur during the drying cycle, use your "stethoscope" described in Chapter Two to pin down the location of the problem for more study. Observe heating performance on all temperature settings. Check to see that a manual timer completes the set cycle before the dryer stops. If not, it may be that the dryer is overheating and has triggered the automatic safety control.

*Access to parts.* How easy is it to remove the service panel? Surprisingly, many buyers can spot potential problems by looking for an orderly unbroken arrangement of parts and insulation. Rust, chipped surfaces, worn or slack belts, and lint accumulation all indicate a lack of past care and point to future repairs.

*Drum rotation.* When absolutely impossible to run the dryer, at least check drum rotation by hand. It should revolve freely without any "play," which generally indicates worn bearings; however, if garments have become jammed between the drum and the frame, they may cause similar problems. Should you hear grinding noises while rotating the drum, look elsewhere for a dryer.

*Electrical connections.* Check for sound insulation on both cord and plug. Connections at the appliance terminals should be secure as well.

*Lint trap.* Check the lint trap and cleanliness of surrounding dryer cavity. You can learn much about past maintenance at this point without even removing the service panel. A heavy lint accumulation in a dryer not only presents a serious fire hazard but it interferes with the free movement of rotating parts, thus shortening appliance life. If the blower, belts, motor, and drum are kept clean and free of lint, a dryer will last many years past the average life expectancy.

# 4

# portable appliances

Secondhand portable appliances are sold through fewer outlets than the major appliances. New surplus portables, other than the occasional sale of discontinued models, are almost nonexistent. Salvage outlets, secondhand shops, and personal sales are the buyer's major sources of supply. Of the available portables, heating appliances tend to be less complicated in design and easier for the average buyer to check than the motor driven appliances. However, a use-test will expose many of the problems of both types. In all cases, "try before you buy" is sound advice.

A two- to four-week portable appliance exchange privilege is common in salvage stores. Many have their own repair departments where they check equipment for grounded circuits, temperature calibration, and a variety of other defects. In these cases, some minor repairs are made. One of the most prevalent problems found in used portables is that of shock potential. Generally, the buyer with a little knowledge of electric wiring can make most of these fairly simple repairs. A number of good appliance repair books can be found in a library, many of which can help the average person without a mechanical background make a variety of repairs. Several such books are listed under "References."

General condition and cleanliness of all small appliances should be checked; it is nearly impossible to clean a really neglected portable cooking appliance. In addition to cleanliness, check the fit of lids and other parts. An electric frypan with a warped lid is a poor investment, as is a coffeemaker with parts bent out of shape. When purchasing any heating appliance, check handles to see if they are conveniently designed. Do the handle and base afford sufficient insulation to protect the server and the table or counter where it rests? A poorly insulated coffeemaker can quickly ruin the finish on your table.

Secondhand portable appliances can be especially good buys for the family that wants an appliance even though the expected use will be very small. A new roaster-oven used only a few times each year is a fairly large investment and, in terms of frequency of use, probably not a very wise one. In many homes, the same may be true of large coffee urns, deep fat fryers, griddles, and pressure cookers. While secondhand portables are often not as attractive as their new counterparts, if well selected they still can give years of service. In surveying the secondhand market, it appears that many homemakers give less care to these portable appliances than to the more costly major equipment. In addition, the non-durable quality of many manufacturers' finishes contributes to the frequently poor appearance found in many after several years of use.

When buying any portable with a detachable cord, check the appliance terminals at the point where the plug is inserted. If they are pitted, it is a likely indication that the owner has been connecting the cord to the appliance after the plug was inserted into the wall outlet. This poor habit causes arcing and subsequent carbon deposits on the terminals. The increased resistance to the electric current will shorten the appliance life span. Even more important, the practice is unsafe. Always connect the cord to the appliance first, then to the source of power.

Appliance wattage requirements give some information as to speed of heating or capacity of a motor driven appliance. Table 4—1 lists common wattage ranges for selected small appliances. However, it is important to remember that many other factors contribute to appliance efficiency and consumer satisfaction. The total design, selection of materials, and quality of construction are all vital to this satisfaction.

**TABLE 4–1**
*General wattage requirements of selected portable appliances*

| Appliance | Wattage Range | Appliance | Wattage Range |
|-----------|---------------|-----------|---------------|
| Blender | 300 – 1200 | Mixer, portable | 100 – 150 |
| Table broiler | 1000 – 1650 | Mixer, stand | 100 – 250 |
| Can opener | 60 – 150 | Roaster-oven | 870 – 1650 |
| Coffeemaker | 450 – 1500 | Table range | 100 – 1650 |
| Frypan | 1000 – 1500 | Toaster | 750 – 1650 |
| Griddle | 1250 – 1600 | Waffle baker | 650 – 1400 |
| Iron | 900 – 1200 | | |

## PORTABLE HEATING APPLIANCES

Check any open coil heating elements for broken wires or those that
have been repaired in the past. A secondhand heating appliance is not
a good buy when the element has been stretched and then reattached
to a terminal screw after a break. The electric current flowing through
the appliance circuit will rise with the resulting lowered resistance
level and the coil will burn out more quickly. Incidentally, such open
heating coil repairs are easy for even the most non-mechanically
minded. Coil replacements are inexpensive and readily available
through a variety of outlets. See Chapter Seven for installation directions.

When possible, thermostatic controls should be checked for
accuracy before buying. And while it is possible to adjust a thermostat by varying the distance between the contact point, expect some
price compensation for your willingness. In the case of detachable
probe tube controls, replacements generally are available unless an
appliance is quite old. These replacements are often not inexpensive.

### HOT PLATES

Most hot plates available from salvage and secondhand shops are of the
older open coil type. The successor to this appliance is known today
as a buffet range. Since January, 1970, all nichrome heating elements

must be covered if they are to have Underwriters' Laboratories approval; therefore, these models will probably begin to appear in the surplus market as well.

Care is needed to avoid electric shock when handling such appliances. Since current flows directly through these coils as it does through a toaster, avoid touching them with a kitchen knife or similar conductor. Small space heaters with much the same construction can also be found in the same shops. The cost of either should not exceed one-third that of a new appliance, and in many instances will be even lower.

## ELECTRIC SAUCEPANS AND DEEP FAT FRYERS

Many of these appliances are given to salvage shops because of infrequent use. Pressure saucepans given away for similar reasons can also be found in these outlets. Many can be excellent buys if you have the need and sufficient storage space. Many homemakers buy pressure cookers yet never use them, in large part because of the lack of confidence or skill. In other cases, the pans go unused because of inconvenient storage – "out of sight, out of mind." The price of a secondhand electric saucepan, pressure cooker, or deep fat fryer should never exceed one-third that of a new appliance. Frequently these pans will be priced even more economically.

### General Buying Guidelines

Sturdy and well balanced construction, well fitting lid

Heat resistant handles and base, easy-to-grasp knob on cover

Generous, well balanced, easy-to-empty fryer basket

Temperature control that is easy to adjust and read

Immersible construction with plug-in cord

Easy-to-clean finish and design

### Surplus Appliance Check List

*Temperature calibration.* Is it accurate? Does the boiling point of a
    water sample coincide with the $212^O$F. setting on the temperature

selector? Test in this manner, increasing the setting until water will maintain boiling level. Such a test will give an idea of the calibration accuracy without a thermometer. To test at higher temperatures, use oil and a deep fat thermometer. While difficult to test before purchasing, the thermostat should be checked before any exchange period has expired.

*Cleanliness.* The cleaner the better. Some saucepans are in spotless condition, some have layers of burned-on grease that are impossible to remove. Commercial appliance cleaners may be of some help in loosening the soil, but prevention of the problem is really the key.

*Missing or worn parts.* Oftentimes the wire basket for deep fat frying is in poor condition, or worse, missing entirely. In some instances, basket replacements can be found in hardware stores or through a parts distributor; in other cases, the size and shape needed may be difficult to find. Usually older pressure saucepans need new gaskets. These are readily available from the manufacturer or a parts supplier since they must be replaced regularly during normal use as well. Buy two to save time.

*Warping.* The heavy gauge metal used in most of these pans discourages warping, but inspect any secondhand pans before buying to see if the bottoms are flat.

## IRONS

Since the life of a steam iron given little or no care averages three years, secondhand irons are questionable buys. Mineralization of steam vents is a major problem, although some newer irons are designed for ease in cleaning these areas. While steam iron condition is doubtful in the surplus market, almost-new dry irons that have been donated because of consumer preference for the steam and spray feature can be found in salvage stores.

Compared to other portable appliances, prices are low for secondhand irons, averaging 10 per cent of the new appliance price. However, poor general quality is a major drawback. The all too common habit of dropping an iron also contributes to this general poor condition.

## General Buying Guidelines

Well insulated handle, comfortable to hold

Firm, wide-base heel rest that will prevent tipping

Controls that are easy to read and set

Sole plate designed to facilitate ironing around buttons

Some method of cord strain relief to prevent excess wear

Easy-to-fill water opening in steam irons.

## Surplus Appliance Check List

*Vent condition.* To check vent condition, fill water chamber of steam iron and heat at a moderate setting. If rusty water spurts out, or, even more ominous, if nothing happens, the ports are probably clogged and it would be well to look elsewhere. Clogged vents can be cleaned to some extent by filling the water chamber with vinegar or a commercial demineralizing solution and heating.

*Electric connections.* Bring your continuity testlight when shopping as used irons have a tendency to develop grounded circuits. If possible, inspect connections at the iron terminals. However, irons are not the easiest appliances to dismantle and each manufacturer seems to have his own unique method of assembly. When circumstances permit, unscrew the removable portion at the back of the handle to expose the electrical connections. If wires are broken, look elsewhere for a used iron.

*Temperature control.* While certainly not an accurate measure of temperature, a few drops of water sputtering on the sole plate surface indicates the iron is heating. A rough estimate of temperature might be borrowed from outdoor barbeque enthusiasts, who claim that if you can hold the palm of your hand near (not on) the source of heat for four or five seconds, the temperature is approximately 300°F. This would approximate the temperature setting just between silk and wool on an iron. While a surface thermometer would give a more accurate reading, these are generally not found in most homes. However, they are moderately priced and would be useful to include in your tool chest for times when a similar temperature problem arises.

*General condition.* The exterior condition of an iron is easy to evaluate. Inspect the sole plate which should be relatively free of scratches, or at the very least, without rough metal burrs that snag fabrics. The handle and temperature dial should be in sound condition without any cracks that would indicate poor treatment on the part of the previous owner. Cleanliness is another indication of past care and maintenance.

## COFFEEMAKERS

Serviceable used coffeemakers are available in the surplus market, but if you're looking for a shining chrome server to grace your company table, you're wasting your time. However, for those interested in performance alone, good buys do exist. Salvage shops receive a few good pots from families with duplicates. Prices are generally low, averaging 20 per cent of the new cost. Large coffee urns can be excellent buys in view of the infrequent use they receive, and often can be purchased for under $5. Since these urns are generally donated to salvage shops because of the storage space required, consider your own cabinets first or the pot may make a round trip.

### General Buying Guidelines

Needed capacity; electric coffeemakers work best when near full

Well balanced design with drip-proof spout

Comfortable, heat resistant handle and easy-to-grasp knob on cover

Easy-to-clean finish and construction

Legible cup measurement indication marks

Automatic keep-warm setting

Fast perking action

### Surplus Appliance Check List

*Temperature setting.* Automatic coffeemakers, regardless of type, always keep coffee below boiling (between 185$^{\circ}$F. and 200$^{\circ}$F.)

since higher temperatures result in bitter brew. Whenever possible, fill the pot with water and run it through a cycle, checking the temperature with an immersion thermometer at the end of the cycle. The automatic keep-warm element should maintain serving temperature after the perking stops.

*Perking action.* If the water in the coffeemaker heats but no perking occurs, a defective pump is a likely cause. It is either jammed or has lost its sealing capacity. When parts are bent slightly, they may be straightened, but pitting is a more difficult problem and is especially common in aluminum pots. The washer on the pump in Figure 4–1 (p. 78) should move freely and fit the bottom of the well. If pitting has occurred in the pump area, the coffeemaker is a poor choice.

*Water leakage.* Cracks in the plastic base or temperature control indicate past problems and if any sign of water leakage can be found, look elsewhere.

*General condition.* Check the fit of lid and spreader as well as the valve stem. From a safety standpoint, it is important that the coffeemaker lid be securely attached. Cleanliness is important when selecting a secondhand coffeemaker because a heavy build-up of coffee oils is difficult or impossible to remove.

## TOASTERS

According to the best estimates available, a new toaster should last about 15 years; when purchased secondhand, eight years. While many modern toasters have more sophisticated controls than those of their predecessors, the older, less complicated toasters were fairly trouble-free and easier to repair.

The usual toaster found in the secondhand market is a simple pop-up model with a mechanical timer. However, a few toaster oven units are beginning to appear in newspaper classified ads. Used toaster prices generally range from 10 to 25 per cent of the new model cost. You can still find used models in salvage shops for under a dollar, which is encouraging these days. If you'll be satisfied with a toaster that simply toasts bread, the used market has many good buys at low prices.

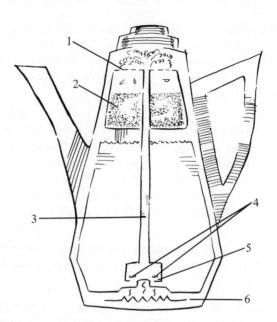

1. Spreader plate     4. Washer valve
2. Coffee basket     5. Pump chamber
3. Tube               6. Heating element

**Figure 4–1** *Pump action on a typical automatic coffeemaker*

**General Buying Guidelines**

Capacity suitable for family needs

Size of bread slots

Shape and size necessary to fit storage area in your kitchen

Easy-to-clean surfaces and construction with hinged crumb tray

Well insulated base and handles

Controls that are accessible as well as easy to read and use

**Surplus Appliance Check List**

*Electric element condition.* Whenever possible, remove cover and
    check condition of heating element. No breaks or stretched wire

should be visible and all insulation should be sound. If electricity is available, check to see that coils or ribbon element will heat.

*Bread carriage or pop-up mechanism.* It should pop up! However, if binding occurs, remove the side panels and clean and oil. This simple maintenance works wonders in most cases.

*General cleanliness.* Look at the crumb tray. It should look as if it has been cleaned occasionally.

*Cord.* Check both cord and plug for soundness of insulation and connections. A new cord will often be needed.

## FRYPANS

The buyer in search of a serviceable used electric skillet will find an ample supply in the surplus market. Many are offered for under $5 at salvage shops. However, utility rather than beauty is the standard for secondhand electric frypans. Some salvage outlets check thermostats for accuracy, but a lack of accurate calibration remains one of the major problems with these skillets. Fairly new and attractive pans can occasionally be found at garage-type sales. When available, these are your best buys.

### General Buying Guidelines

Capacity to suit your needs; sizes vary from 8½ inches to 15 inches in diameter

Removable heat control allows for complete immersibility

Heat resistant handles and base; easy-to-grasp insulated knob on cover

Well fitting frypan lid with secure exhaust vent shield

### Surplus Appliance Check List

*Temperature control.* To check temperature calibration, add an inch or so of water and set the control dial to $212^\circ$F. Water should boil at this setting, although you will probably need to cover the pan to reach this temperature. Remember, too, that in normal use the current regulated by the thermostat cycles "on" and "off," causing the temperature to vary by about 25°F. The signal light will indicate the "on" cycle.

*Heating element and electrical connections.* Frypan heating elements are enclosed inside the bottom of the pan and are impossible to inspect. However, if the appliance terminals are visible, check for any pitting which would indicate a carbon build-up at the connection and thus greater resistance to current.

*Appliance cord.* If the appliance cord accompanies the frypan, inspect insulation for soundness. If it does not or is in poor condition, consider this added cost as part of the purchase price. Should the appliance plug differ from the sizes commonly available in hardware stores, think twice about the purchase since ordering a special cord from the manufacturer may pose problems in availability, delay, and cost.

### ROASTER-OVENS

Portable roaster-ovens are large and can serve as a substitute or supplement for a range oven. Though they appear infrequently in salvage shops, they may be offered through the newspaper classified ads. When available, roaster-ovens can often be purchased for less than $10. These appliances tend to have less chrome and expendable trim than many portables. Consequently, secondhand roaster-ovens suffer less surface damage than many of the smaller cooking portables. Roaster-ovens, like large coffee urns, are often resold because of the space requirements, so consider your own storage space before buying.

The relatively high wattage required by roaster-ovens indicates the need for an independent electric circuit, or at least one free from other appliances when the roaster is being used. For safety and performance, do not use an extension cord in addition to the appliance cord when cooking.

### General Buying Guidelines

Adequate insulation with heat resistant handles and base

Sturdy, easy-to-clean construction and finish

Capacity in relation to family needs.

Well fitting cover with adjustable steam vent

Rust and stain resistant rack

Removable cooking well with easy-to-grasp handles

## Surplus Appliance Check List

*Temperature control.* To check calibration use an oven thermometer, comparing temperature against that indicated on the dial.

*Wiring condition.* If possible, inspect the wiring at the terminal screws either before purchasing or, if there is a return privilege, immediately thereafter.

*General condition.* Check racks, inner porcelain lining, and exterior finish for rust or scratches. Be sure to remove the interior lining during your inspection.

## WAFFLE BAKERS AND GRIDDLES

Waffle bakers and griddles are similar in basic construction and waffle grids are oftentimes reversible, serving both functions. Personal sales and salvage outlets are the best sources to check for these appliances. Prices should not exceed one-third the cost of a new model.

### General Buying Guidelines

Capacity and type to suit family needs

Automatic signal light to indicate which waffle is ready

Expansion hinge on waffle baker

Easy-to-remove grids with a grease drainspout

Durable, easy-to-maintain construction and finish

Closely set, high knobs give a crisp waffle; low, widely spaced construction, a softer product

### Surplus Appliance Check List

*Cleanliness.* The cleaner the better. To be honest, however, you should expect some carbonized grease residue on both waffle baker and griddle.

*Electric element and connections.* The waffle baker with its open coil wiring located under the grids is one of the easiest appliances to check for past repairs. The construction is much the same as a hot plate or toaster in this respect. Before buying, remove waffle grids and inspect the heating element. If the spring-like coil is broken, no electricity will flow through the circuit, thus no waffles. Chapter Seven tells how to make this repair but a lower price tag should reward your efforts.

*Connecting cord.* The cord between the upper and lower elements must be sound. If broken, it can be repaired much as an extension cord but heating will not occur until the circuit is complete.

*Appliance cordset.* Check cord connection. A secure plug with no bare wires and unbroken insulation indicates a sound cord. Both grease and heat will soften a rubber cord so check insulation carefully to avoid future problems.

*Temperature control.* Plug the waffle baker or griddle in to see if the grids or surface will heat sufficiently to cause a drop of water to "skitter" across the surface. At the same time, check the indicator light, if present, to see if the electricity cycles on and off. If not, the thermostat is probably not in working order.

## MOTOR DRIVEN PORTABLE APPLIANCES

As with any appliance, check such obvious features as exterior and interior condition, cleanliness, condition of cord, plug, and wiring if possible. Turn the motor shaft by hand. If it turns freely with a minimum of "play," bearings are sound. Whenever possible, remove cover plates surrounding the motor and control. You will be surprised at how much you can discover by looking for a clean and orderly arrangement of parts; the amount of flour and dust particles found inside many mixer heads is surprising. If the interior surfaces of motor driven appliances are cleaned occasionally, the reward will be years of extra service.

Many motor driven portables are "lubricated for life," but *whose* life is subject to question. It is best to clean out and replenish lubricating grease after a time. Sluggish starting or sparking of universal motors such as those found on mixers may be due to worn carbon brushes. In this case brushes will need to be replaced. Gummy accumulations of oil and dirt or weak springs are other causes of slow starting intermittent operation. To lubricate bearings, use S.A.E. No. 10 or 20 oil, making sure none is applied to the motor windings. Many such maintenance tasks and small repairs take little technical skill, just common sense. Efforts here pay dividends in lengthened service life.

## MIXERS

Both portable and stand mixers can be found in salvage outlets with years of service life remaining. Both sell for prices ranging from 10 to 25 per cent of the new cost. When looking for a stand mixer, search personal newspaper classified ads. Generally, appliances offered here are in better condition than those sold through other outlets.

Scratches and the absence of bowls are common problems with secondhand mixers. Suitable bowls can frequently be purchased separately or bowls already owned can be substituted for those missing. To be safe, check to see whether a special size or shape bowl will be required when buying a used mixer.

### General Buying Guidelines

Motor with mechanical governor or solid state feedback control to hold speed constant regardless of load

Shift lever for correct bowl replacement

Easy-to-clean beaters and mixer; smooth non-staining materials and finishes

Number of speeds needed for flexibility

Well balanced; stand-type needs base stability; portables should be easy to hold

Firm beater retention catch; easy ejection when desired

Convenient controls unlikely to be adjusted by an accidental movement

### Surplus Appliance Check List

*Beater blades.* Sometimes beaters are sold separately in salvage outlets, but do try them in the mixer before buying. When searching for a replacement beater blade, bring the broken one along to compare size and shape. Many of these can be found for as little as 10¢ in salvage stores.

*Grounded circuits.* Portable mixers are especially susceptible to unintentional grounds to the appliance housing. Always check for a grounded circuit with a testlight as discussed in Chapter Two. A vibration or "tingle" felt when your hand touches the mixer body or switch indicates a serious safety hazard. While some salvage outlets check for continuity and these unintentional grounds, it is a good idea to recheck yourself just to be sure.

*Speed selector.* Plug in the mixer, checking to see if the beater blades rotate at different speeds when the selector is turned to a higher setting. When your purchase carries a return privilege, test by beating foods of different consistencies, watching for any lag action. Ideally, a mixer should not overheat when beating a heavy batter. But don't expect to beat stiff cookie doughs with a lightweight hand mixer either!

## BLENDERS

Fewer blenders than mixers can be found in salvage shops partly due to the relatively recent expansion of the market. However, the introduction of more sophisticated controls will probably encourage new purchases, making the earlier models available in the used market. Quite a few used drink mixers can be found but remember that these are not versatile blenders and should be limited to blending liquids. To be of good general use, a blender must have at least two speeds. More than two really does not add to its utility. Since the minimum markdown you should expect on a used blender is one-third that of the current new price, it will pay to check current models before searching in the used market, as prices have dropped in the last few years and sellers are often reluctant to adjust to the actual market level.

### General Buying Guidelines

Ease of cleaning, removable blades, and smooth construction with a minimum of crevices

Instant "on" and "off" control as a safety measure

Well balanced assembly with weighted base

Convenient controls with at least a "high" and "low" speed selection

Container with convenient spout for pouring

**Surplus Appliance Check List**

*Cover.* Check for warped condition of plastic covers. Dishwashers sometimes distort, making the seal less than effective.

*Motor base assembly.* Although the blender motor is fairly well protected, look for signs of water leakage.

*Blade assembly.* Check for bent blades and the general fit of this assembly.

*General condition.* Gaskets can be replaced and you should probably expect to do so. Check for exterior cleanliness and condition.

*Use-test.* Whenever possible, try all speeds before buying, listening for any unusual noises. Remember few blenders are quiet.

## KNIFE SHARPENERS AND CAN OPENERS

Both are often combined in one appliance or, if sold separately, the internal mechanisms are quite similar. The average homemaker opens 900 to 1500 cans a year, so if an electric can opener is to be a timesaver, it must be easy to operate. Sometimes electric openers go unused in favor of a well constructed manual can opener which sells for only a few dollars. Actually, an efficient manual tool may provide greater convenience in many kitchen situations.

Unfortunately, the can openers given to salvage outlets seem to be those of less convenient design. Good knife sharpeners are even more difficult to find in the used market and they often have mechanical problems. However, a few good models are resold partly due to manufacturers' tendencies to combine small appliances in a single package. Often knife sharpeners are donated to salvage outlets when a family purchases a new electric can opener complete with duplicate knife sharpener.

## General Buying Guidelines

Durable construction with easy-to-maintain finish

Removable can opener cutting assembly for easy cleaning

Sturdy design to prevent accidental tipping

Magnetic lid holder

Opener that rolls cut edges on cans for safety

### Surplus Appliance Check List

*Use-test.* Take a few empty clean cans closed on one end when shopping so that you can try any can opener that appears suitable. Clean edges without metal shavings are a must. While a dull cutting blade could be sharpened with emery cloth, the price should be very low if this is the case.

*Electric circuits and connections.* Be especially careful to check for grounds to the appliance housing. Shock potential is a common cause for the discard of these appliances. Check plug and cord for sound insulation.

*General condition.* Check overall cleanliness, condition of sharpening stone or cutting wheel.

# 5

# floor care equipment

There are over 50 makes and models of vacuum cleaners on the market. The vacuum's utility for cleaning carpeting is fairly well established; however, with the use of attachments, it can handle many additional above-the-floor cleaning tasks with equal ease. Regardless of the model selected, attachments properly used and maintained can shorten cleaning time. Dust draperies, lampshades, and fabric-covered walls with the soft dusting brush attachment. Clean the hard-to-reach areas in upholstered furniture with the crevice tool. These or other attachments can be used to remove cobwebs from the ceiling or dust on floor moldings with less bending and reaching than would be required otherwise.

Before selecting any vacuum cleaner, new or used, list the necessary cleaning tasks in your home that can be lightened with proper floor care equipment. Next, decide which model will best handle these needs. A canister model is generally superior for above-the-floor cleaning and the care of hard surfaced flooring. In most cases, the upright vacuum provides superior rug or carpet cleaning results. The choice may be a difficult one and we might wish for both types. If need, storage, space, and budget permit, you might consider buying two serviceable used vacuum cleaners, one upright and one canister, rather than a single new model. The combination provides flexibility not found in a single cleaner at about the same price as a new upright model.

Secondhand vacuums might serve special needs other than general household cleaning. One very practical application for an older canister vacuum is in a home workshop area. With very few adaptations, it could be connected to a power sander, thereby eliminating to a great extent the problem of flying dust particles. The same vacuum cleaner can be used to dry paint in half the time when you move the hose to the exhaust side of the appliance. The tack rag, used to remove surface dust from wood before finishing, can be all but eliminated with the use of a vacuum. Try it next time you sand a piece of furniture.

Other floor care appliances, such as floor polishers, scrubbers, and rug shampooers, also can be found in the used market. While these serve well in many home situations, every family will not have the need or wish for them. For example, before buying a carpet scrubber, consider your willingness to assume this new cleaning job. It may be that you really are happier hiring an outside rug cleaning firm when needed. However, if you have much carpeting in your home, a rug shampooer can save your family considerable money over the years. Another factor is the availability of storage space for this infrequently used equipment.

In some instances, home scrubbers are not as desirable as the commercial cleaning processes. A rotary brush is damaging to oriental-type rugs and fairly ineffective when cleaning deep shag rugs. Actually, the shags are more decorative than practical in terms of cleaning. Regardless of construction, carpet manufacturers caution that the normal detergent residue left following home cleaning tends to attract soil. Therefore, carpets will need to be cleaned more often than when professionally steam cleaned.

Floor scrubbers and polishers facilitate housework you probably already do, either by hand or with rented equipment. While few home-makers would disagree that a floor polisher is a most functional appliance for buffing waxed floors, many would question the need for a floor scrubber. And they would be right in many cases. The additional equipment cleanup time can far exceed any initial energy savings. However, when larger floor areas are involved, a scrubber can expedite a tiresome cleaning job. Because of the similarity of construction, many polishers also can be used to scrub floors and shampoo carpets.

## UPRIGHT VACUUM CLEANERS

Upright vacuums clean by means of strong suction aided by motor driven brush action. The revolving brush separates the rug pile for better pickup. Supplementary attachments are required for hard surface or above-the-floor cleaning. Normally the basic tools — floor brush, upholstery nozzle, dusting brush, crevice tools, extension wands, and hose — are included in an attachment kit. While the attachments can add another $25 or more to the cost of a new vacuum cleaner, with most secondhand models they are included as an extra that does not add substantially to the price. However, when buying a used vacuum, don't be surprised to find a few of these attachments missing. Tools have a way of getting lost when used infrequently. Since attachment styles change infrequently, most can be replaced by writing the manufacturer. However, if you appreciate a bargain and do a bit of searching, missing tools often can be found at a salvage shop for under a dollar.

### Availability and Cost

While relatively few vacuum cleaners are traded in at retail outlets at the time of a new purchase, a reputable appliance store is still a good outlet to check for a secondhand cleaner. Before shopping, a word of explanation is in order. The description "rebuilt" indicates that a vacuum has been completely overhauled, one hopes with a new bag and hose added. The work "reconditioned" implies that badly worn parts were replaced and the machine put in satisfactory working order. Guarantees on rebuilt machines usually include necessary labor and parts covering any breakdowns occurring within one year of purchase. Remember, a parts-only guarantee means less to the consumer because, with the exception of the motor assembly, vacuum cleaner parts can be fairly inexpensive to purchase but expensive to install.

Personal newspaper classified ads are usually the best source of serviceable and inexpensive used cleaners. While no worthwhile guarantee accompanies such items, vacuum cleaners are less complex to test than most major appliances. A simple use-test can uncover most major problems and a few sellers will refuse to let you run the cleaner. Even with a new vacuum, demonstrations are far more prevalent than with other equipment. A selection of older cleaners can often be found in salvage shops, where good buys exist if you are willing to make a few repairs. But try before you buy.

While vacuum prices vary widely depending upon age, manufacturer, and condition, $30 to $40 seems a fair price to pay for a serviceable rebuilt cleaner. Others can be found for even less if you are willing to replace a stretched belt, repair the cord, and do some cleanup work. Paint is frequently chipped but since this is a strictly utilitarian appliance and usually not seen except by the user, perhaps this problem could be overlooked if an especially good buy is found. Fortunately, rust is less of a problem with vacuum cleaners than with those appliances which involve heating elements or water. However, for appearance's sake, appliance paint can be used to touch up nicks and scratches in the exterior finish.

### Service Life Expectancy

The service life expectancy of a new upright cleaner is 18 years; for a secondhand cleaner, eight years. With proper care, a vacuum can be one of the home's most durable appliances. However, the motor's worst enemy, dirt, is a clear hazard in floor cleaning equipment. A primary filter or bag, and in many instances, a secondary filter act as a guard to protect the motor assembly. Both should be securely attached and clean if they are to do their jobs. While tempting from a budget standpoint, it is not a good idea to re-use the disposable vacuum bags because of the reduced air flow through the dust clogged bag surface.

### General Buying Guidelines

Whether buying a new or used upright vacuum cleaner, consider the following features when making your selection:

*Motor.* A relatively quiet motor is highly desirable, and sufficient power is needed for adequate cleaning.

*Maneuverability.* An upright cleaner should be easy to move with a convenient handle, adjustable for vacuuming under furniture. A low motor housing helps here also.

*Cleaning tools.* Tools should be easily assembled, convenient to use, and scrubbable in soapy water when necessary.

*Cord storage.* Some form of cord storage is desirable. Select an upright with either an automatic rewind or hooks for manual storage.

*Controls.* The "on-off" control should be easy to reach. It is most frequently in the handle or, if a toe switch, near the cleaner head.

*Bumper guards.* Guards of soft rubber or plastic are necessary to prevent marring furniture when vacuuming.

*Bags.* The bag should be convenient to change. Disposable bags greatly simplify the dirt disposal problem. An indicator that warns when the bag is full can be found on some cleaners.

*Brush adjustment.* A high-medium-low brush adjustment makes a variety of carpets easy to clean and adds versatility.

## Surplus Appliance Check List

When searching for a surplus upright vacuum cleaner, consider the following guidelines:

*Use-test.* Run the vacuum under actual cleaning conditions. A vacuum is far easier to test in a home or store than other appliances. When demonstrating a cleaner, salesmen tend to use only those materials easily picked up with suction alone. Prepare for a more realistic test by bringing a few common dirt samples of your own. A good cross section includes grass clippings, threads, cornmeal, soda, and oatmeal — all readily found at home. These simulate the different forms of surface litter a cleaner will be expected to pick up in the average home. A well constructed, properly maintained cleaner should pick them all up with ease. If the rug used in testing has been laid over somewhat resilient padding, an upright vacuum, when picking up oatmeal, will cause particles to bounce if the brush is touching the carpet at the correct point. If this vibration does not occur, check brushes at the bottom of the cleaning head for wear or lack of proper adjustment.

*Maneuverability.* While making your use-test, check to see if the upright cleaner is easy to move back and forth under low pieces of furniture. Check the handle adjustment levels for ease and stability. The vacuum is one of your most portable of appliances and it should move with as little effort as possible.

*Brushes.* For proper cleaning the brushes should touch the carpet. Brush adjustments are possible for various carpet constructions, but generally speaking, when brushes no longer touch the edge of a piece of cardboard laid across the nozzle opening, it is time to change them. In some cleaners, a 1/32 inch clearance is allowed. See Chapter Seven for instructions on this repair.

*Bag.* A too-full bag also causes problems in pickup performance. For best cleaning as well as motor protection, bags should be changed when about half full.

*Motor Noise.* Quiet is the word. If the cleaner picks up the suggested dirt samples and has a quiet, smooth running motor, chances of a large repair bill in the near future are almost nil. While difficult to see because of the motor and fan enclosure, bent fan blades are a frequent cause of noisy operation. When bent, the fan creates less suction, thus reducing cleaning ability.

*Cord.* About 20 feet of rubber or plastic covered cord with insulation intact is what you want. This is the most prevalent defect you will find when looking at vacuum cleaners offered for sale by private families. It is easy to run over non-retractable cords when vacuuming, cutting through the insulation layers. Inspect cords, looking for any glints of bare copper wire showing through the insulation layers. These exposed conductors are a severe shock hazard, but if the selling price is low, you might want to make the easy cord repair or replacement yourself. If not, the cleaner will have to be serviced before it can be safely used.

*Appliance plug.* A heavy-duty plug designed so it can be easily grasped is needed. Constant tugging on the cord rather than the plug will loosen wires from the plug terminals. See Chapter Seven for repair directions if a new plug is in order.

*Drive belt.* Check the belt attached to the brush and motor shaft, looking for hair, strings, and other debris which indicates a careless previous owner. If the belt is worn or stretched, replacement is easy and inexpensive. This is a common repair that will be necessary from time to time. When buying from a private seller, ask if he has any spare belts as these will probably not fit his new cleaner, and an extra belt can save you a trip to the store.

*General cleanliness.* Operating a vacuum with an overly full bag, clogged hoses, or secondary filter will cause the motor to work harder than necessary, overheat, and allow dirt build-up in the fan chamber. All these conditions lead to early retirement.

*Attachments.* Check ease of assembly and general efficiency in use. Some models require an adapter attached under the bottom of the vacuum head, which makes moving the cleaner from place to place more difficult. In these cases, attachments are less useful.

## CANISTER OR TANK VACUUM CLEANERS

A canister or tank cleaner is usually needed when more smooth flooring than carpeting exists in a home. The variety of available cleaning nozzles are a help in caring for above-the-floor surfaces and generally require less effort than those attached to an upright cleaner. In most cases, the canister or tank design depends wholly on suction and a more powerful motor is used than in those models where a combination of suction and agitation exists.

### Availability and Cost

The same outlets handling upright vacuum cleaners carry canister models. Beware of the door-to-door salesman who advertises rebuilt models at unbelieveably low prices, arrives with a new "much more suitable" cleaner, and shows great reluctance when asked for a demonstration of the advertised model. "Bait and switch" advertising is all too prevalent in vacuum cleaner and sewing machine merchandising.

Good serviceable canister or tank models can be found through the classified ads for less than similar cleaners offered through retail outlets. However, those sold privately do not carry a guarantee. Appliance dealers offer rebuilt models with some guarantee covering parts and labor at about half the new price. The motor is frequently guaranteed for one year, but be sure to check the duration of any agreement before buying.

### Service Life Expectancy

The average life of a new canister vacuum cleaner is 15 years. Again, care as well as initial design is the key to the life span. Since floor care equipment is stored out of sight after use and the user is generally tired when finishing with housecleaning, it is easy to understand why the vacuum receives so little cleaning and servicing until absolutely essential. But preventive maintenance is the key to long service.

## General Buying Guidelines

Many of the same features desirable in the upright cleaner pertain to the tank or canister models. In addition, consider:

*Ease of movement.* Since canister cleaners are carried from place to place, good balance is essential as well as a comfortable case handle.

*Floor brush instruction.* Equal suction is needed along the entire length of brush. This is especially vital since cleaning in this instance largely depends on high suction.

*Cleaning tools and wands.* Positive locking devices for tools, wands, and hose to eliminate slipping are highly desirable. Wands should fit closely together.

*Tool storage.* Convenient storage on the cleaner itself eliminates extra trips for needed brushes.

### Surplus Appliance Check List

To check cleaning efficiency of a canister vacuum, make a use-test with the same dirt samples mentioned in the upright cleaner section.

*Nozzle construction.* While construction of cleaning heads differs, a firm seal between nozzle and carpet is important with a canister or tank model since suction is usually the principal cleaning action. However, the homemaker can defeat the best designed cleaner with poor handling. Unlike the upright vacuum, some effort on her part is required to maintain this nozzle-carpet contact, although good equipment design can make this easier.

## LIGHTWEIGHT HAND VACUUMS

While considered by some to be convenient for dusting, a hand vacuum should act as a supplement to, rather than a replacement for, an upright or canister-type cleaner. Few are found in the used market except through an occasional newspaper classified ad, garage, or other personal sale. Most families that own hand vacuums tend to keep them even when not often used because of the very low resale value. If you find a hand vacuum, chances are it will have much service life remaining because of the relatively few hours of use, and have a low price.

## FLOOR POLISHERS, SCRUBBERS, AND RUG SHAMPOOERS

Many new floor polishers will also scrub hard surfaces and carpets. Personal newspaper advertising is the major source of supply for secondhand floor care equipment. Although it is possible to find a few surplus polishers or scrubbers at the time of a major model change, this occurs less frequently than with most kitchen and laundry appliances. When available, used models will be frequently offered for about one-quarter or even less of the price of new equipment.

The usual alternative to buying a new polisher or shampooer is rental on a daily or hourly basis when this irregular housecleaning task occurs. Such maintenance equipment is available through many hardware and grocery stores as well as conventional rental outlets. The cost of renting a domestic-sized shampooer or polisher is modest. However, in some cases the user must buy a specific liquid shampoo for the rug cleaner which adds somewhat to the overall cost. Actually, most detergent and water solutions work as well as the more costly commercial shampoo, and this savings might figure in the decision to rent or buy.

### General Buying Guidelines

Except in the case of a fairly old model, a floor polisher is seldom just a polisher. The brushes are used for scrubbing carpets or rugs, for wax removal, floor washing, and even sanding. When buying either a new or used polisher-scrubber, check:

*Maneuverability.* Balance is essential when choosing these appliances. At best, scrubbers or waxers are difficult to guide because of normal vibration. The closer a polisher-scrubber can come to floor moldings the better.

*Brushes and pads.* Different models have a variety of brushes, pads, and special polishing attachments. Even steel wool and sanding disks are available for special tasks. Ideally, all should be easily attached and fit securely.

*Water or wax container.* When present, the tank should be convenient
  to fill and empty, as this is a fairly messy task at best.

**Surplus Appliance Check List**

When looking for a used polisher-scrubber, check the following
features before making a selection:

*Brushes.* Never store a polisher or scrubber resting on its brushes.
  When this has been done, the brushes will be flattened and the
  cost of replacements should be calculated as part of the purchase.
  Inspect the polishing pads as well, although more than likely
  you should expect to replace these.

*User manual.* A rug shampooer-scrubber-waxer is a fairly complicated
  appliance and most users refer to the manual for all except
  simple buffing, so try to secure these instructions when purchasing.
  If you are fortunate enough to get the owner's copy, check to
  see that you receive all the accessories. Brushes and scrubbing
  pads, used infrequently, have a way of getting lost.

*Cord and plug.* Both should be sound. Where water is used, there is
  a double hazard of shock.

*Exterior condition.* This is another appliance that users mistreat.
  Polishers and scrubbers are seldom used and should give long
  service with care. Inspect the bumper guards that protect woodwork. Remove the scrubbing and polishing brushes so you can
  look closely at the shafts. All attachments should fit securely or
  else they may fly off in use.

*Noise and vibration.* While all are somewhat noisy in operation, the
  shafts holding brushes or pads should rotate fairly smoothly.
  Try before you buy, avoiding any equipment that jerks, shows
  excessive vibration, or changes its normal motor hum.

# 6

# sewing machines

If we were to rate equipment found in the average home in terms of ability to stretch the family budget, most of us would put the sewing machine near the top of the list. Possessing even modest skill, the home sewer can make draperies, table linens, clothing for the family, plus a whole host of other practical and decorative items at a fraction of the cost of ready-made goods. While economy has frequently been one of the major motivations for home sewing, it has also become a creative outlet for those interested in individualized fashions and furnishings.

In a commercial sense as well, few inventions have had such impact in the industrial market as the power sewing machine. With it came the entirely new concept of the mass produced, ready-to-wear garment. The growth of the needlework industry paved the way for the great variety of popularly priced clothing and furnishings that we take for granted in today's market.

The selection of a sewing machine is far from simple. First the consumer must decide whether a straight stitch or zigzag machine is needed and then whether a portable or cabinet model is more desirable. Next she must select from among the many options available in decorative stitch features and other special attachments. Coupled with the problem of design complexity is the buyer's general inexperience in choosing a sewing machine. The equipment life expectancy is long, and in general, few models are purchased in a consumer's lifetime. Perhaps these reasons partially account for the questionable merchandising methods that are all too frequent in the sewing machine market. While many honest, dependable retailers exist, the consumer still needs to be aware of the many common fraudulent selling practices.

The Better Business Bureau warns the prospective buyer to avoid marketing tactics that border on fraud. Salesmen sometimes make a special offer, "good only for today." while rushing the buyer into a contract before he has time to check the machine thoroughly or compare prices of other equipment. Other merchandisers offer free gift certificates which apply to the purchase of equipment with prices conveniently inflated before the "special offer." Beware, too, of contest drawings where, by coincidence, everyone seems to win second prize, entitling him to a "free" sewing machine head. In these instances, the price of the mandatory cabinet purchase comes as quite a surprise. In other cases, the machine may be offered totally free, but a long-term service contract is required before collecting your "gift."

Few newspaper classified sections checked did not carry at least one ad for a new zigzag sewing machine at an unbelievably low price, warning in some instances that the sale was on a first-come, first-served basis. Chances are that when the salesman arrives at the consumer's door, it will not be with the advertised bargain but with a "much better machine, that is obviously more suitable. . ." at about $200 more than the advertised model. This is not to say that actual sewing machine bargains do not exist; however, the selection of a reputable dealer is a necessity.

### Availability and Cost

New and used sewing machines are sold through a variety of outlets: company-owned retail stores, mail order firms, department stores, large dry goods outlets, salvage shops, and also by private sellers. The prices vary considerably depending upon age, condition, accompanying attachments, whether straight stitch or zigzag, and style, whether cabinet or portable. The availability of replacement parts is naturally one of the greatest price determinants. Question seriously the purchase of any machine where parts are not readily available; for the lack of a simple bobbin case, your would-be bargain will simply take up space.

A reputable dealer who does his own servicing is the most reliable source to check when searching for a good new or used sewing machine. When buying a reconditioned sewing machine from a dealer, look for at least a year's guarantee on parts and labor. In some instances, two years' service accompanies the purchase. Obviously, the longer the guarantee, the better. A parts-only guarantee is inadequate protection as labor costs will constitute the major expense in almost all sewing machine repair situations. A ten-year-old sewing machine that has been thoroughly reconditioned generally sells for about half the price of comparable new equipment.

Private sellers advertise secondhand sewing machines at about half the normal dealer price. These are sold "as is" without any reconditioning or reliable guarantee. However, in some instances they may be excellent buys, especially for the consumer who sews infrequently. When considering such a purchase, test carefully and inquire about the availability of parts before purchasing.

Prices of new sewing machines vary widely from under $100 to over $400. The more mechanically complex the machine is the higher the initial cost. In addition, equipment offering many options in stitching tends to have a more costly repair record. Modern sewing machines are much more versatile than their forerunners and can facilitate a great many sewing tasks. However, many owners fail to make use of the attachments or special features even though their addition to the basic machine can add several hundred dollars to the total price. Therefore, before buying a top-of-the-line sewing machine that can stitch a whole host of decorative patterns, darn, ruffle, and handle dozens of other sewing tasks, take inventory of your own needs. Once this decision has been made, you are ready to shop either the new or used market with greater confidence of satisfaction.

## Service Life Expectancy

The 24-year life expectancy figure for sewing machines was established before the introduction of today's more complex equipment and therefore can serve only as a very rough guideline for consumers. While newer models have become much more complex with the addition of zigzag stitching and countless other decorative or functional variations, a sewing machine is still one of the most durable pieces of household equipment found today. Pennock and Jaeger found that a used electric sewing machine might be expected to provide the second owner 16 years of service.[1] Even a used treadle machine was expected to function satisfactorily for 13 years. Such potentially durable equipment merits a consumer's careful consideration before purchasing in order to assure long-range satisfaction.

A sewing machine's life is undoubtedly extended by the relatively light use it receives in most homes. The average domestic sewing machine is used far fewer hours than any major appliance found in the home. In all likelihood it also receives better care and maintenance than many appliances. A dirty machine will readily soil light-colored fabrics, and if a sewing machine is not oiled regularly, the results are quite noticeable to even the most lax owner.

While the addition of many of the newer automatic features has increased repair needs and costs, in all fairness it should be noted that the versatility and usefulness of the sewing machines has also increased. We now mend, appliqué, embroider, make buttonholes, and sew on new stretch fabrics — tasks that would have been difficult or impossible on most of the older machines. However, to make full use of your purchase, a user's manual is probably more essential than with almost any other piece of equipment. Not only does the sewer need a constant reference for the many adjustments needed for specific tasks, but since a sewing machine is often unused for months at a time, the most routine jobs — like threading a bobbin or adjusting tension — may require the help of a user's manual. Ask for it and then keep it in a convenient spot near the machine.

### General Buying Guidelines

*Quality of stitch.* A well balanced straight stitch is vital whether sewing on a lightweight fabric or heavy wool. Test all machines and avoid any that either stagger or skip stitches. Machine tension should be easy to adjust. For ordinary stitching, the upper and lower threads should be locked in the center of the fabric as shown in the following diagram.

[1] Jean L. Pennock, Carol M. Jaeger, "Household Service Life of Durable Goods," *Journal of Home Economics* (January, 1964), p. 23.

Tensions balanced

Upper tension tighter than lower

Upper tension looser than lower

*Ease of threading.* Machines with open guides tend to be easier to thread than other models. When testing, thread the machine yourself, evaluating the convenience. Next, wind the bobbin, observing how easily it can be taken out of the case and replaced. You will have to do this many times while sewing and some bobbin constructions can be frustrating to even the most skillful.

*Starting action.* Sewing machines should start slowly without any "nudge" from the operator, thereafter running at the desired speed.

*Smoothness of parts.* Run your finger along the presser foot and the edges of tension disks to test for any surface roughness that can snag fabric or break thread. Precise machining and smooth finishing during manufacturing are vital in sewing machine construction.

*Balance of machine.* If the machine head must be tipped at an angle in order to change a bobbin or clean under parts, the overall balance of equipment and cabinet becomes increasingly important. Check this feature before buying.

*Controls.* Should all be easy to read and adjust. Look for controls that do not need constant adjustments. Both knee and foot speed controls are available and many machines have both. An infinite speed selector providing a full range of motor speeds gives the sewer greater control when working on complicated tasks than a machine having only two motor speeds.

*Reverse action.* Check smoothness of reverse action, if applicable, watching carefully for any tangling bobbin thread.


**Surplus Appliance Check List**

When looking for a used sewing machine, in addition to considering the general buying guidelines, check the following details:

*Use-test.* Bring several samples of fabrics that you commonly use for sewing for the use-test. Demonstration fabrics used by salesmen tend to be those easiest to sew on. When testing, check the adjustments and threading mentioned.

*Availability of parts.* Are they currently in stock? This is one of the most important questions to ask a reliable source. And, sad as it may be, not all sellers are truthful in this respect.

*Cleanliness.* Inspect all working parts for any signs of neglect.

*Cabinet construction.* If a cabinet model, check construction. Are the hinges sturdy, legs well braced, and leaf well supported?

*Guarantee.* When buying from a dealer, the sewing machine should be thoroughly reconditioned and carry a parts and labor guarantee for at least one year.

# 7

# appliance repairs
# and maintenance

Any appliance, new or used, requires proper maintenance and generally some repair to remain in top working condition. While most major work is better left to a competent appliance serviceman, there are a few commonly needed repairs that the average owner can handle with confidence if he wishes to save money. In addition to these repairs, a number of general use and care suggestions have been made that can in some instances lower your utility costs, and in others, lengthen the life of household equipment. In addition, since safe use is such an integral part of appliance education, certain precautions have been emphasized.

## SIMPLE REPAIRS

Directions for seven commonly needed repairs for household appliances are given in this chapter. Even if you wish to attempt only the first two — repair of appliance cords and plugs — the savings in service expense would be pleasantly noticeable in your budget. Another consideration is the time and the human tendency to put off repairs that are not absolutely mandatory. Ragged insulation or a broken plug do not necessarily halt appliance operation, yet do constitute a serious safety hazard. Often the time needed for repair will be far less than that required to take a portable appliance to a service center.

### Appliance Cord and Plug Replacement

One of the major problems we found when checking small secondhand appliances that were offered for sale was a defective cord or plug. Ragged cord insulation was also common on many floor care appliances. Rigid plastic plugs crack fairly easily and the service cost for replacement is often high in relation to the original appliance price.

Actually, replacement of cords or plugs on most portable appliances is a simple repair requiring only a screwdriver, knife or scissors, and a few inexpensive parts. Major appliances and some of the more heavily powered portables require larger wire and heavier insulation but the repair itself is very similar. In some appliances, a third or ground wire often is added for safety. The ground wire is connected to a corresponding grounding prong on the male or convenience outlet plug. Whether you repair any defective plugs and cords on future secondhand purchases or simply repair your present appliances as needed, a considerable savings in the family budget will be evident.

*Convenience outlet (male) plugs.* A variety of these plugs exist, all performing the same job — that of bringing electricity from the outlet to an appliance or light fixture. These plugs are commonly made of plastic or rubber and most frequently have the conventional two prongs, each of which is connected to a terminal screw or substitute connection. Some plugs have an additional third (or ground) prong which minimizes the serious shock potential should the body of the appliance become electrically "live." While some plugs can be repaired and re-used when in sound condition, others molded around the terminal screws must be cut off and thrown away when repairing a defective cord. In these cases, buy a new plug and connect it to the cord as suggested.

When buying a replacement plug, it is important to know what is available and be able to select the one best suited to the job at hand. Most hardware or electric supply shops carry five different plugs that are fairly all-purpose. Others are sold for special installations or heavier equipment requiring individual hookups. When buying an electric plug or wire be sure to look for the UL seal denoting Underwriters'

Laboratory approval for safety. The most common plugs used in the home are:

1. Three-pronged grounding plug. This requires a ground receptacle for maximum safety rather than an adapter plug. A three-wire cord is used in this installation and it is vital to connect the ground wire to the corresponding prong.

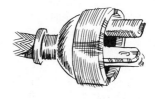

2. Heavy-duty plug with metal brace. The brace is added for greater strength. It is frequently used with power tools either outdoors or in basement shop situations where an ordinary plug might be crushed or damaged by impact.

3. Molded plug of plastic or rubber. While some have removable inserts which allow wiring repairs at the terminal screws, most must be cut off and thrown away when the adjacent wire or plug connection becomes defective. However, a new plug may be attached if the cord is still in good condition.

4. The most common plug.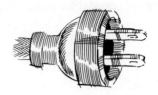
   The extension for easy grasp
   which discourages tugging on
   the cord makes it safer to use
   than (5). An insulation insert,
   sold with the plug, should be
   slipped over the ends of the
   prongs to cover exposed conductor wires twisted around
   the terminal screws. The soft
   rubber plugs are more durable
   than most rigid plastic plugs.
   While they may not be as
   generally attractive, they are
   more resistant to impact, which
   is common when using lighting
   fixtures, portable appliances,
   and floor care equipment.

5. A plug similar to (4) but with-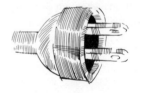
   out the easy-to-grasp extension.
   This design encourages tugging
   at the cord when unplugging,
   which loosens the fine copper
   wires, frequently causing a
   short circuit. In brief, it is a
   poorly designed plug.

MALE PLUG REPLACEMENT DIRECTIONS

Before attaching the male plug to an appliance cord, first cut off all
defective wiring, squaring wires so both sides are even. When insulation
is broken, the wire must be cut beyond that point. If this results in a
too-short cord, buy a new one of the necessary size and length, replacing connections at both ends.

1. Thread cord through plug as shown, gently separating the two wires at this end for a distance of about 1½" without removing the insulation surrounding each.

2. If space allows in the plug construction, tie an underwriters' knot as shown, allowing enough wire to extend above the knot so that connections can be made at terminal screws in the plug.

3. Remove 1/2" insulation from the end of both wires. Use a knife, scissors, or wire stripper made especially for the job. Take care to remove only the insulation and not break the individual wire conductors. When a woven fabric layer is used as the outside covering in a multiple insulated cord construction, cotton thread tightly wrapped at the cut edge can eliminate fraying.

4. To secure the cord to the male plug, twist each bundle of conductor wires tightly in a clockwise position, forming a small U-shape with each bundle that will fit around the two screws. Position under each terminal screw in a clockwise position (the same way the screw tightens) and tighten. Be sure all wire strands are under the terminal screws as shown.

5. Slip insulation cutout over prongs and check for a short circuit with your battery test light.

*Appliance cords.* When replacing an appliance cord, it is important for safety and maximum electrical efficiency that you use the correct size wire and type of insulation. Appliance cords can be found with wires ranging in size from AWG No. 6, for use with a heavy-duty appliance such as a range, to AWG No. 18, for lower wattage rated appliances or lighting fixtures. The length as well as the diameter of wire and surrounding insulation is important.

When replacing a cord, use the same size wire and type of insulation as previously included by the manufacturer. When selecting an extension cord, either for use with lamps or appliances, consider these same factors. Many appliances, especially those rated over 1000 watts, are designed to be connected directly to a wall outlet and not used with an extension cord. When this precaution is ignored and conventional small wire extension cords are used, voltage drop occurs and wires overheat, creating a safety hazard. While voltage drop lowers the efficiency of all appliances, it is more damaging to motor driven equipment. When sufficiently lowered, the motor tends to labor and may burn out.

If you must use an extension cord, the following table will help.

TABLE 7−1
*Guide for 120 volt extension cord selection*

| | AMPERES (From Name Plate) | | | | | | | | | |
|---|---|---|---|---|---|---|---|---|---|---|
| | 2 | 4 | 6 | 8 | 10 | 12 | 14 | 16 | 18 | 20 |
| *Extension cord length* | | | | | *Wire size (AWG)* | | | | | |
| 25 ft. | 18 | 18 | 18 | 18 | 16 | 14 | 14 | 12 | 12 | 12 |
| 50 ft. | 18 | 18 | 16 | 16 | 14 | 14 | 12 | 12 | 12 | 10 |
| 75 ft. | 18 | 16 | 14 | 14 | 12 | 12 | 10 | 10 | 10 | 8 |
| 100 ft. | 16 | 14 | 14 | 12 | 12 | 12 | 10 | 10 | 8 | 8 |

The proper insulation is also important in appliance cord selection. The insulation surrounding the conductors protects a user from electric shock. The most efficient type varies, depending upon conditions of use and equipment construction. Cords in common use include:

Light-duty rubber or plastic covered cord. Often found on lower wattage portable appliances and lighting fixtures.

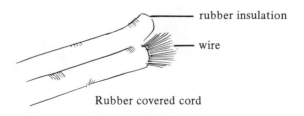

rubber insulation

wire

Rubber covered cord

Heavy-duty cords with multiple layers of insulation and an outside fabric layer. These are often found as permanently attached or detachable cordsets used with roaster-ovens, irons, waffle bakers, and higher wattage heating appliances.

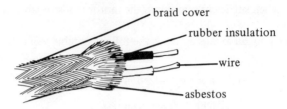

braid cover
rubber insulation
wire
asbestos

Heating appliance cord

Heavy-duty rubber (or rubber-like composition) cords with multiple layers of insulation. These are commonly found on tools or appliances where resistance to both moisture and mechanical injury is important.

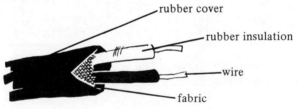

rubber cover
rubber insulation
wire
fabric

Heavy duty rubber covered cord

Three-wire appliance cords. The insulation may vary but multiple layers are frequently used in this construction.

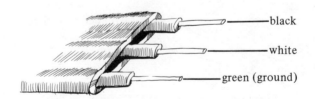

black
white
green (ground)

Three wire appliance cord

*Appliance (female) plugs.* In some instances, electric cords are attached permanently to appliances; in others, such as the immersibles, a detachable cordset may be used. Actually both constructions are quite similar with regard to electrical repair. Whether the cordset wires terminate within the appliance itself or a detachable plug, the two conductors are fastened to some terminal connection in much the same manner as previously described. When connecting irons and the higher wattage heating appliances, special lugs or connectors are often used for greater security.

When working with a detachable appliance plug, defective terminal connections can be repaired easily if screws or removable clamps have been used to secure the two halves of the female plug. In some cases, the halves have been riveted together. Unless you wish to drill out the rivets, replacing them with screws, cut off the old plug and begin anew with another. Buy a replacement with screws large enough to fit an ordinary screwdriver. Some require that extra tiny tool we never seem to have, and except for those with the greatest manual dexterity, the accompanying tiny nut severely challenges the repairman's temper.

Detachable appliance plugs are available in several sizes. Before shopping, measure the distance between the projecting appliance connections or, better yet, take the old plug for comparison. In some instances you'll need a special plug that can only be ordered from the manufacturer or a parts distributor, but most replacements can be found in an electrical or hardware store.

FEMALE PLUG REPLACEMENT DIRECTIONS

1. Always disconnect any cord from an outlet before attempting a repair.

2. Disassemble plug, checking the placement of each part. Remember — you must reassemble too.

3. Cut both wires squarely at a point above damaged wire or insulation. If remaining cord is too short, purchase a new length, replacing connections at both ends.

4. Remove about 2½" of outer covering as shown, wrapping cotton thread or electrician's tape tightly around edges to reduce fraying of a fabric covered cord. This is not required of plastic covered cord.

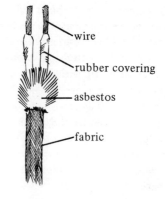

wire

rubber covering

asbestos

fabric

5. Thread cord through spring protector so that free ends are in the position for terminal screw attachment as shown.

6. An underwriters' knot may be tied for added security if space permits. However, when the spring protectors shown are used, this need has been eliminated to a great extent.

7. Remove about 1/2" inner insulation from the end of each wire conductor bundle.

8. Twist each group tightly in a clockwise direction, forming a U-shape. Connect both under the terminal screws as shown.

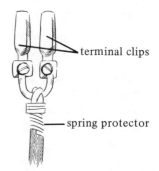

terminal clips

spring protector

9. Fit terminal clips and protector spring into one half of the plug in appropriate depressions and replace screws or clipping device.

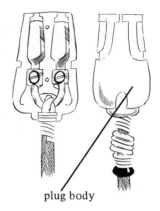

plug body

10. Check for possible short circuits with your battery testlight before plugging into an appliance. Attach one test lead to one prong of the male plug and touch the metal body or second lead of the testlight to the other prong. If the testlight glows, a short circuit exists.

**Portable Appliance Heating Coil Replacement**

Small heating appliances have been produced with both open and enclosed heating coils. The open coil type can be repaired or replaced quite easily and inexpensively. Buy heating coil replacements from the original manufacturer, appliance parts dealer, electrical supply, or hardware stores. Bring the old coil when shopping as it is important to buy the same size element. If a break in an open coil element occurs next to the terminal screws, repair may be possible without replacement. First clean the wire and terminal screws thoroughly by gently scraping with a dull knife to remove any carbon or corrosive deposits. Next, reattach the heating element to each of the terminal screws as shown in Figure 7-1. Tighten screws firmly so that electric current is carried efficiently.

When a break occurs other than directly adjacent to a terminal, remove the old element, replacing it with another of the same size. Position the new coil under the insulators in the same manner as the original element, attaching each end to a terminal screw as above.

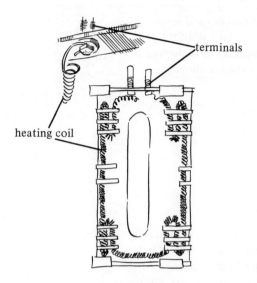

Figure 7 — 1  *Heating coil replacement*

## Upright Vacuum Cleaner Brush and Belt Replacement

In most upright vacuum cleaners, roller brushes should be replaced when they no longer touch the edge of a piece of cardboard laid

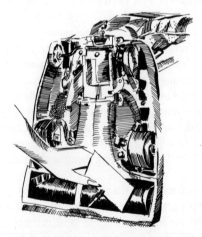

**Figure 7 — 2**  *Checking upright vacuum cleaner brush condition*

across the nozzle opening as shown in Figure 7—2. Check the user's manual for specific instructions as some models are designed to allow a slight gap between these surfaces. New brushes are available from the manufacturer or parts distributor.

While vacuum cleaners vary in construction, most brushes can be removed and replaced as follows:

**VACUUM ROLLER BRUSH REPLACEMENT DIRECTIONS**

1. Remove bottom plate from upright vacuum cleaner.

2. Unlatch or unscrew the roller brush holders and remove the drive belt.

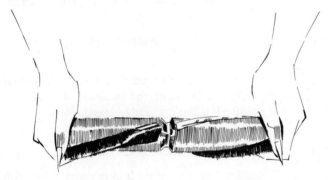

3. Remove the brush roller and unscrew or pry off the metal end caps holding the brushes in the roller.

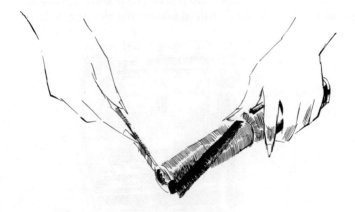

4. Ease worn brush inserts out with a screwdriver or similar tool.

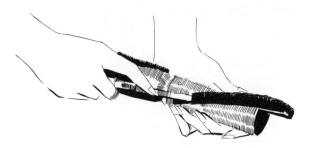

5. Slide replacements into the same openings, making sure gaps in the brush line up with bars on cover plate.

6. Replace belt and insert assembly in position, replacing roller holders.

7. Be sure brush roller rotates with forward pull. If not, remove belt from motor shaft, give it a half twist, and try again. It is easy to forget the belt position if a user's manual is unavailable.

UPRIGHT VACUUM BELT REPLACEMENT DIRECTIONS

1. Remove any remaining fragments of the broken vacuum drive belt. The model number of the cleaner is your best shopping guide for proper replacement size.

2. Remove vacuum brush roller and replace belt in correct position. (If you're lucky, the user's manual will describe this position.) In

Belt at roller end

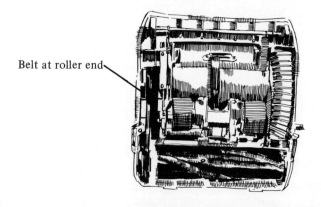

some instances, the belt is attached to one end of the roller; on others, the belt is centered, fitting into a groove designed for this purpose. Belts may need a figure eight twist or fit in a straight loop position.

Belt in center

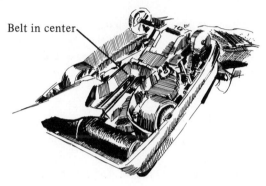

### Refrigerator Gasket Replacement

When the refrigerator door gasket no longer seals tightly, it is time to replace it. It has been suggested that if a firm gasket seal exists, a piece of paper the thickness of a dollar bill can be withdrawn from between the door and the adjacent surface only with a determined tug. This test may be a bit demanding, but if you can feel cold escaping around the door, without question the time has come to replace the gasket.

Measure the old gasket and check the appliance model number. You will need this information when buying a replacement from the manufacturer or an appliance parts distributor. When you buy the new gasket, remove the old one by loosening the screws that hold it to the door and replace with the new strip. New gaskets for freezers, washers, and dishwashers are also available and can be installed in an almost identical manner at fairly low cost.

### Cleaning Steam Iron Ports

The ports and water chamber of a steam iron may clog after a year or two of use if water with heavy mineral deposits has been used. Vinegar, a mild acid, can be useful in dissolving alkaline lime deposits found in the vents and valves. Fill the water chamber of the iron with white distilled vinegar, plug in and steam for two minutes. Next, allow the iron, still filled with vinegar, to stand overnight. In the morning, empty and rinse several times with clear water. You may expect a vinegar odor during the first few uses, but this will gradually disappear.

A few words about preventing such deposits in the first place: distilled or de-ionized water will stretch the life of any steam iron. And while some designs facilitate the cleaning of the chamber and ports, this is still sound advice.

## MAINTENANCE PRACTICES

### Refrigerators

Clean condenser whenever needed and at least once or twice a year. Dust acts as an insulator, inhibiting heat exchange. To compensate, the motor runs longer, shortening its life span and using more electricity in the process. Use a long handled brush or vacuum cleaner attachments. As a safety precaution, unplug the refrigerator before cleaning.

Build up a worn door gasket temporarily by padding with clear plastic wrapping between the two layers. For best results and lower utility costs, replace the old gasket whenever possible. (See "Simple Repairs" section for directions.)

Stop interior odors before they start. Tightly cover all strong-smelling foods before storing. Wipe up spills immediately to save both time and effort as well as to discourage odors. Deodorize and clean the food chamber using two tablespoons of baking soda and a quart of warm water. Baking soda is a mild abrasive that will not scratch porcelain enamel and cleans efficiently whether used as a powder or in solution.

Wax the refrigerator cabinet several times a year after a thorough cleaning with mild detergent or soap and water.

Insist on level installation — it is vital to long and trouble-free motor life.

Lengthen life by proper location. Whenever possible, avoid locating a refrigerator or freezer next to the range or in a niche. The higher ambient temperatures will lengthen motor running time and shorten service life expectancy.

### Freezers

The same maintenance suggestions appropriate for refrigerators also serve freezers as well. In addition:

Disinfect the defrost drain with boiling water after thoroughly washing with detergent and water. Some homemakers then swab with chlorine bleach to further discourage bacterial growth. This procedure will keep any appliance with a similar drain opening sanitary.

Freeze less than 10 per cent of freezer food capacity at one time. Larger quantities take more time to freeze, and in the process, larger ice crystals are formed which destroy the original texture.

Remember to clean the freezer. Because of its nature, we often forget that a freezer, too, needs regular, thorough cleanings both inside and out.

### Dishwasher

Clean the sump and strainer area, where debris can collect, whenever needed. Just how often depends on your thoroughness in pre-rinsing dishes before loading.

Take care when loading that smaller pieces don't slip into the wash arm mechanism during the cycle. Be especially careful when loading tools or flatware with pointed handles. These often fall just far enough through the silverware basket to damage the wash arm below.

Wash the appliance cabinet with mild detergent or soap and water when needed. Check the door and opening flange area which are not self-cleaning to the same degree as the interior wash chamber. Protect the cabinet several times a year with appliance wax.

Scrub wood top if used for a cutting board; then sanitize and rinse well to guard against food poisoning. A little mineral or salad oil will help retain the finish. Sanding and refinishing will remove deeper scratches and discolorations. Wood tops when used as cutting surfaces require considerable care and may not be worth the effort.

## Water Heaters

Insist on level installation for maximum service life. Heater legs or base should be adjustable to compensate for sloping floors common in many basement installations.

Protect water heater tank and at the same time ensure a clean water supply by flushing out iron and lime deposits regularly. Do this by opening the drain valve at the bottom of the tank for a few seconds. Incidentally, this practice will cut your heating bill as well.

Regulate water temperature as needed. While both clothes and dish-washers require water between 140°F. and 160°F. for best performance, temperatures above this range are damaging to water heaters. When a heater is set at a higher temperature to compensate for losses sustained when water is piped long distances, a second heater placed near these appliances may be economical.

## Ranges

Keep clean inside and out. Spills are much easier to wipe up as they occur, and while this is impossible when the oven or top surfaces are hot, soil doesn't become easier to clean as time goes on. For stubborn spots, soften overnight with a dish of ammonia and a cloth. Let the cloth act as a wick, spreading ammonia slowly over oven spills. Next morning you will be able to clean more easily. Rough abrasives like steel wool or coarse cleaner may be tempting but they will permanently scratch the enamel finish.

Use aluminum foil with the greatest of care. Actually, it would be better if you avoided this practice completely. Protecting drip pans or the oven bottom with foil is a risky practice from the stand-point of safety, the food, and your range. When laid under the oven element, foil can cause a short circuit at the terminal block and in some ovens it is possible for the foil to fuse to the bottom. While some use and care books sanction the practice, it is still of doubt-ful safety.

Rotate the use of surface units as you do the spare tire on a car for longer service life. To preserve utensils and lower utility bills, use the large unit only when cooking in large saucepans, kettles, or skillets. The pan should match the size of the surface unit.

Loosen soil on oven racks or any non-aluminum parts without scrubbing by soaking in ammonia and water for a few hours. Even stubborn burned-on grease comes off easily. If the size of oven racks poses a problem in your kitchen sink, soak in a large laundry sink, plastic wading pool, or as a last resort, the bathtub. As when using any toxic cleaner, keep ammonia out of the reach of children and pets.

Clean enamel surfaces with mild soap and water as needed. Allow the range to cool slightly before washing or enamel surfaces may "craze"; that is, develop tiny cracks in the surface. Actually, modern porcelain finishes are quite resistant to temperature changes and are vastly improved over the earlier thick coatings. Damage is far less prevalent than in earlier appliances. To prevent stains, immediately wipe up any acid foods which may etch the finish. If an abrasive is needed for stubborn spots, baking soda is an effective but gentle cleanser. To ease future cleaning and provide added protection, polish about once a month with appliance wax.

Drain gas burners by turning upside-down after washing. They should be thoroughly dry before replacing.

Check gas burners for proper adjustment. A correctly adjusted flame has an inner blue cone. The presence of any yellow indicates incomplete combustion and the need for burner adjustment. While fairly simple adjustments are possible on some gas ranges, others require a repairman. Burner adjustments are often made on a complimentary basis by the gas utility for its local customers.

## Clothes Washers

Turn off water supply valves whenever a machine is not in use to eliminate any pressure on the intake hoses. This practice lowers maintenance costs and protects your laundry area from unexpected flooding in the event a connecting hose bursts.

Open the washer door after laundering so that the wash tub and gasket have a chance to dry thoroughly. It is a poor practice to leave wet laundry in the wash tub for an extended period, both from the standpoint of the equipment and the wash.

Remove the agitator post in top loading machines for periodic cleaning. Sand, threads, and other accumulations can scratch washtub surfaces or bind the agitator.

Level all automatic washers to eliminate excessive vibration that would greatly shorten service life.

Measure the amount of detergent accurately rather than adding by the "dump" method. This is as important for the life of the equipment as the laundry. Check the user's manual to see whether low sudsing detergent is suggested. Front loading washers are especially vulnerable to suds blocks.

Clean exterior surfaces when needed with non-abrasive cleaner or mild detergent. For added protection, polish several times a year with an appliance wax.

Avoid spilling laundry additives such as bleach or fabric softener on the enamel surfaces. Should a spill occur, wipe up quickly to avoid staining the finish.

Check lubrication requirements for wringer washers. In many instances, the wringer head and motor have oil holes which require two or three drops of motor oil each month. Proper lubrication will lessen excessive wear at these points.

Observe water level indicated inside the washtub or on agitator parts of non-automatic washers. When a washer is filled beyond this capacity, the excess water may drain into the gear case causing damage.

Avoid unbalanced loads as well as overloading in all machines. However, this caution is especially important when using an automatic washer. Curiously enough, a very light load, such as a single pair of filmy curtains, can cause unbalancing as readily as a single heavy item. To add years of service to your automatic washer, take heavy rugs or other large items to specially designed coin operated machines or a commercial laundry.

Rinse and dry wringer rollers before storage to preserve the rubber. Resiliency will be prolonged if you release the pressure after laundering.

**Automatic Dryers**

Clean the lint filter after every use. At least once a year, unplug the
dryer and vacuum the cavity between the interior tub and outer
shell using the vacuum crevice tool to reach remote areas. (FOR
SAFETY, BE SURE TO UNPLUG THE DRYER BEFORE CLEAN-
ING.) Not only does lint slow dryer operation, but more important,
a heavy accumulation often causes overheating. This combination
of highly combustible lint plus excessive heat can result in open
flames that travel through the entire venting system. Destruction
can result if the fire is not checked in time.

Unless otherwise instructed by the manufacturer, vent the dryer
to ensure proper thermostatic response, safety, and sanitation.
Outside venting also keeps walls and windows in the laundry
area dry.

Clean cabinet and interior drum occasionally with mild soap or
detergent and water. At the same time, wash the lint filter with
suds and hot water. Wax the cabinet several times a year to
protect the finish.

Avoid using the top surface for stain removal. While a handy
surface for such jobs, the enamel can become cloudy and dis-
colored when exposed to certain chemicals.

Do not overdry laundry for its sake, the dryer's life span, and your
budget. Reducing drying time when using a 4000 to 5000 watt
appliance will go much further in cutting your utility bill than
turning out a 100 watt light bulb occasionally.

**Vacuum Cleaners**

Empty the bag when about half full. Re-using the disposable bags,
although tempting, is dubious economy. Air must escape
through pores in the vacuum cleaner bag and even a thin coating
of dust can build up a felt-like layer inside this container,
lowering the cleaning efficiency.

Wash the secondary filter occasionally, if one is present in your
vacuum. This filter, more often found in upright cleaners,
additionally protects the motor and fan assembly in case dirt es-
capes from the bag, which is the primary filter.

Replace brushes on the upright vacuum agitator roller when necessary or cleaning will be incomplete. Manufacturers' directions vary, but all brushes should be fairly close to the level of the nozzle. See "Simple Repair" section for replacement directions.

Avoid running a cleaner over its cord while vacuuming to protect the insulation layers. When storing, wind the cord loosely around the hooks provided for this purpose to avoid damage to the wire conductors.

Clean the exterior and interior surfaces when needed, giving special attention to hose-bag connection, which occasionally becomes clogged with dirt. Wash the plastic or metal shell with soap and water, using appliance wax occasionally. Wash brushes and vacuum attachments in sudsy water, rinse, and dry thoroughly before using again.

Turn the cleaner off before disconnecting from the wall outlet. Resist that impulse to tug at the cord rather than bending to grasp the plug itself. Terminal connections are often loosened this way.

**Floor Polishers and Scrubbers**

Lengthen the life of brushes by washing before they accumulate a heavy coating of wax. Rinse and dry thoroughly before the next use.

Clean floor or rug scrubber tanks thoroughly after each use; rinse and air dry. While it is tempting to put off this somewhat tedious cleanup chore when you are tired, fight the impulse.

Hang polishers and scrubbers on a hook in a convenient dry place. They should never rest on their brushes in storage; equipment weight is damaging to the bristles.

**Small Heating Appliances**

Repair cracks in plastic bases with putty-type epoxy. This material is resistant to water and has the same insulation qualities desired in the base or handles of these appliances. Application is easy and it dries speedily.

Beware of the still-warm range element when plugging a small appliance such as a coffeemaker into the range convenience outlet. Should the cord inadvertently touch a hot surface element, many things will happen — all bad. You will completely ruin the range outlet, short the small appliance, and have an electric fire in the bargain. When using the range convenience outlet to start the morning coffee, be sure the appliance cord is in a safe position.

Connect the electric cord or probe tube control to the appliance BEFORE plugging it into a wall outlet. This safety habit can prevent a serious accident caused by an electrically "live" cord. It could save a child's life.

Clean all appliance surfaces as soon as possible after using. A general cleaning guide for base materials and finishes has been included at the end of this section.

Remove any crumbs from heating elements with a soft brush AFTER unplugging the appliance.

Let small appliances cool before washing or soaking. Metals warp and porcelain enamel may craze when subjected to a severe temperature change.

Use distilled or de-ionized water to lengthen the life of any steam iron. For home demineralization treatment, see the "Simple Repairs" section. As a safety precaution, always disconnect a steam iron when filling with water, being especially careful not to dampen the cord.

Protect an iron sole plate from scratches by avoiding pins, snaps, or other sharp objects when ironing. Use only detergent and water or baking soda to clean the bottom surface. Coarse abrasives will mar the finish permanently. After cleaning, heat the iron slightly, rubbing over waxed paper while still warm; then polish with a soft cloth.

Avoid toasting sticky convenience foods in conventional pop-up toasters. A toaster's life is shortened considerably when such snacks drip icing or jam into the heating elements. As a safety measure, avoid toasting any foods wrapped in foil. A severe shock can result.

Clean the toaster crumb tray, washing with soap and water frequently. Be sure to let dry before using again.

Protect cord insulation and wires. Never wrap any cord around a warm appliance, as the insulation may soften. Detachable cordsets need space to hang or rest in a loosely coiled position. When bent sharply in a drawer, the fine conductor wires inside the insulation layer tend to break.

**Motor Driven Portables**

Lubricate appliances only where indicated. However, do not add more than a drop or two of motor oil at a time at points of wear. More is not necessarily better.

Avoid overloading a lightweight mixer. While it may whip lightweight batters easily, do not expect a small mixer to beat stiff cooky dough. The motor will overheat and die a quick death.

Examine the grease in the mixer gear case yearly — the front cover is removable in most models. Mixer life will be extended if the old lubricant is replaced every two or three years.

Wash blender blades with care, both to preserve their sharp edges and to protect your fingers. Thoroughly dry the rubber gasket that fits between blade assembly and the container before reassembling. It will reward you with extended life and resiliency. While gaskets are inexpensive, they often must be ordered from the manufacturer, which takes time.

Wipe can opener blades or wheels with a sudsy cloth after each use. Dismantle the appliance frequently for a more thorough cleaning. Food acids eat into the cutting surface, dulling the wheel or blade, and even more serious is the danger of food poisoning from a dirty can opener. When the cutting surface is not removable, a small brush or pipe cleaner with soap and water does a good job.

**Sewing Machines**

Remove pieces of thread and fluff that collect under the needle plate and around the hook as frequently as necessary. Certain fabrics shed more readily than others.

Lubricate the parts of wear regularly, using a fine grade of oil
   specifically sold for sewing machines. However, a drop or two
   in the right spots is all that is needed. Too much oil will make
   surfaces sticky, thus attracting dust. The shuttle race is a
   particularly vulnerable spot. Clean and lubricate frequently.

Secure needle in the correct position; tighten, holding screw
   firmly in place. A loose needle can damage fabric, jam the machine,
   and create a hazard to the operator. Place needle so thread lies in
   the long groove when sewing. If inserted incorrectly, the machine
   will not operate properly.

Clean and oil the stand of a non-automatic treadle machine as well
   as the sewing head. A treadle that does not turn freely usually
   needs oiling. One drop is sufficient at each oiling point.


## GENERAL APPLIANCE CLEANING TECHNIQUES

A general knowledge of the characteristics of materials and finishes
commonly used in appliance construction is necessary to ensure
proper care. A variety of materials can be found on a single
appliance – such as a range – making the task of cleaning somewhat
complex. While a sudsy cloth used regularly will handle most needs,
in some instances other cleaners are needed to banish the more
stubborn stains.


### Aluminum

Aluminum is used extensively in the manufacture of cooking
utensils. However, we also find this versatile metal in many portable
and major appliances. It is frequently used for range reflector bowls
under surface units, and as trim. Because of its excellent conductivity, it is the major material selected for electric frypans, waffle
bakers, and griddles.

Wash aluminum with soap or detergent and water, rinsing with
clear hot water, and polish dry with a soft cloth. Alkalies darken
aluminum; therefore, avoid using ammonia, bleach, soda, or other
strong alkaline solutions when cleaning. To lighten a darkened
surface, apply a mild acid solution. An acid food such as stewed
tomatoes or rhubarb will brighten an electric saucepan, but if these

do not happen to be on the menu, you might boil two teaspoons cream of tartar and a quart of water for the same result. Vinegar works equally well. Soap-filled steel wool pads can be used to brighten aluminum or remove stubborn spots. They scratch the surface slightly but this is usually not highly objectionable except on mirror finishes.

**Stainless Steel**

Stainless steel, as its name implies, is resistant to staining. This material has often replaced chrome finishes in both major and portable appliances. We find stainless used in electric knife blades, waste food disposers, blenders, dryer drums, dishwasher cabinets, range tops, and as component parts in almost all appliances.

Stainless steel seldom needs more than a thorough washing with soap and water, rinsing, and careful drying. If not dried completely, it tends to water-spot, and if overheated, it turns dark or "rainbows." The darkening is generally irreversible, but minor stains are sometimes removed by a light scouring. Special commercial stainless steel cleaners are available and fine steel wool or scouring powder, when used with care, is suitable for most finishes.

As stainless steel is not a good conductor of heat when used alone, electric frypans are usually reinforced at the cooking surface with a metal that will improve this function, such as copper or aluminum. If this is not the case, a low heat will be necessary to reduce the danger of scorching.

**Steel**

Steel is widely used in the manufacture of household equipment. Most major appliance cabinets are steel as well as many appliance parts. While steel is also found in small appliances, plastics have replaced it in many situations. The metal is extremely strong and durable, but it rusts if exposed to moisture without protection. Appliances of steel are often finished with porcelain or baked enamels. Before this application, the more durable equipment is treated to resist rust should the enamel finish be damaged. When cleaning steel appliances, consider the exterior finish, as this will determine the care requirements more than the base material.

## Iron

When we think of this material, our thoughts ordinarily turn to the old familiar cast iron skillet. While cast iron bathtubs, radiators, a wide range of cooking utensils, and decorative ware are still to be found, the material is used less frequently today in the manufacture of appliances. Sheet and cast iron have been used for appliance frames, burner grates on gas ranges, gas barbeque grills, and a few small appliances designed for specialty cooking such as fondue and bean pots.

Iron is heavy and it rusts easily. The uncoated metal requires seasoning when used in utensils. However, in almost all instances when used in appliance construction, iron has been coated with porcelain enamel or paint. The exterior finish will dictate the necessary care in these instances.

## Glass and Glass Ceramic

While glassmaking is an ancient art, modern glass can be formulated so that it resists chemicals, impact, heat, thermal shock, and a variety of other environmental problems. We cook in glass, use it in see-through oven doors, appliance covers, gauges on coffeemakers, and in blender containers. We find glass lighting fixtures in our major appliances, glass backsplash protectors on ranges, and glass shelves in refrigerators.

Glass ceramics, while exhibiting many of the same characteristics as glass, is harder and stronger, more resistant to abrasion, and is completely unharmed by exposure to temperature extremes because of its low coefficient of thermal expansion. Used widely in utensils and tableware, we also find it used in smooth-top ranges, in surface units, and in some portable heating appliances.

Generally, mild detergent or soap and water is all that is needed to keep glass or glass ceramic ware clean. Commercially prepared cleaners are available, ranging from spray cleaners for windows to a cleaner-conditioner with silicone added to protect glass ceramic range tops. Vinegar, a mild acid, will dissolve mineral deposits, and ordinary chlorine bleach is helpful in removing many other stains. If an abrasive is necessary, use a mild one as any glass will scratch. A plastic scrubber is a good choice.

## Copper

Copper is used for ventilating hoods, optional decorative doors on refrigerators and dishwashers, as a finish applied to the bottom of cooking utensils (or as a core) to improve the conductivity of stainless steel, and in the manufacture of specialty cooking portables such as chafing dishes. Generally, when used in appliance construction, copper is protected with a lacquer finish to deter oxidation. When cleaning, a general washing is all that is needed. Harsh abrasives as well as excessive heat will harm this protective finish. Untreated copper may be brightened with commercial products or a homemade cleaner made from vinegar or lemon and salt. Rinse well after cleaning and polish dry with a soft cloth.

## Chromium

Chromium finishes are popular coverings for small appliances such as waffle bakers and coffeemakers. In both brushed and mirror finishes, it is used as trim on many major appliances, as decorator styled doors on certain built-in appliances and in many functional appliance parts. Chromium is a hard metal that requires little more than soap and water plus a thorough drying to keep it shining. Since it is an applied finish, harsh abrasives should not be used. Should the need arise, baking soda is a suitable mild abrasive cleaner.

## Porcelain Enamel

In simple terms, porcelain enamel is glass permanently fused to metal at high temperatures. Most frequently, porcelain is applied to a steel base; however, we also find it covering iron and aluminum. Finishes are often white but may appear in any color desired. Porcelain is more resistant to heat and staining than the organic baked enamels. We find it in self-cleaning ovens where the temperature exceeds $1000^{\circ}$F., inside laundry appliances, refrigerators, and on the top surface of many appliance cabinets, even when the side panels have been coated with baked enamel. Brightly colored porcelain enamel is used on many portable cooking appliances. Water heaters, sometimes labeled "glass lined," have their tank interiors coated with this ceramic finish.

Newer porcelain enamel finishes resist most stains and are far more resistant to crazing and chipping than in the past. The material is basically glass and generally requires no more than regular washing with soap and water. Gentle abrasives such as plastic scouring pads and baking soda are effective in removing more resistant spots. While new, thinner coatings of porcelain can withstand a 500°F. temperature change without crazing, it is necessary to allow the older finishes to cool slightly before cleaning with water. It is always a good idea to remove spills as soon as possible to avoid stains. A periodic cleaning with appliance wax adds protection.

### Synthetic or Baked Enamel

Plastic resin-based enamels in a variety of colors are found as finishes on many major appliance cabinets and also on portables. The finish is sprayed on the base metal, then baked at temperatures ranging from 200°F. to 400°F. Consequently, it is less resistant to heat than porcelain enamel. Synthetic enamels do not chip upon impact but can be scratched. As a whole, they are less stain resistant than porcelain enamel.

When cleaning, avoid abrasives and rely mainly on soap or detergent and water. An occasional cleaning with appliance wax adds luster and protection. It is difficult to tell porcelain from baked enamel just by looking. The Porcelain Enamel Institute suggests that a certain "orange peel" effect showing a slight ripple or pimple effect is visible when looking at porcelain enamel finishes at an angle against the light source. Appliance cabinets may not be completely finished in synthetic or porcelain enamel. Both appear in combination at times, usually with the appliance top surface finished in porcelain because of its greater resistance to stains and scratches.

### Plastics

Plastics are a family of materials with characteristics as varied as the many applications found in today's market. Plastics are available as flexible films, paints and adhesives, opaque or transparent rigid forms, and in many other states, each with varying physical properties. Plastics are light in weight, readily compatible with color, and highly adaptable to mass production methods. We find plastics just about everywhere in the appliance field. Refrigerator and freezer liners, appliance housings, nylon gears, switching mechanisms, protective coverings such as the polyimides, anti-stick finishes such as Teflon, appliance handles and bases, and countless other parts are all made of plastic.

With such diversity, establishing care requirements for the group as a whole becomes an impossible task. We are reasonably safe in relying on soap or detergent and water, avoiding coarse abrasive action wherever possible. Plastic scrubbers developed primarily for cleaning the earlier Teflon finishes are still a good general aid for stubborn spots. It is best to avoid contact with high heats, as some plastics melt while others char upon exposure.

# 8

# home furnishings

Less standardization in price and quality of design or construction can be found in the home furnishings market than in the appliance field. Well proportioned, comfortable chairs can be found for under $25, while others, perhaps created by an outstanding designer, may cost over $500. The selection of accessories for the home affords even greater diversity. Well designed decorative objects may be found in almost any shop, whether dime store or art gallery, and price is not a reliable guide to esthetic merit. In addition to the variety of available consumer choices in the home furnishings field, individual family needs are highly flexible and compiling a list of basic requirements would be a difficult task.

The home and its furnishings is a substantial investment for any family. However, estimates vary considerably, depending on many variables including the age, size, and economic status of the family. One estimate, that of *Modern Bride's* research department, reports the average bride-to-be acquires $3,100 worth of home furnishings during a six-month period.[1] This expenditure includes furniture,

[1]"The Bridal Market," a summary of retail spending caused by first marriages prepared for *Modern Bride* by Ziff-Davis Publishing Company, 1971, p. 3.

appliances, radios and stereo equipment, linens, floor coverings and draperies, tableware, utensils, and decorative accessories.

The surplus or secondhand market offers a variety of furnishings for the home, some of which, when substituted for new goods, could considerably reduce this initial figure yet provide consumer satisfaction. Used purchases may well offer an attractive alternate to the ever-present ads that promise "Three rooms of furniture for the low price of $10 a month." In practice, the payments seem to end just about the time the sofa collapses.

The used furnishings market is broad in price and quality. At one extreme, antiques may cost many times the price of new goods and often are considered an investment that will increase in value. On the other hand, offerings from a family attic or local salvage shop might be considered temporary expediencies to be discarded after they have served their purpose. Between these extremes lies a large group of attractive, serviceable furnishings. Some can be used "as is," some require cleaning, and others need refinishing or reupholstering.

While the term "home furnishings" indicates a broad range of goods used in the home, this chapter will be limited to furniture, certain textiles, and a selection of decorative accessories. Even within these groups, the quality and quantity of used or surplus furnishings is varied. Secondhand furniture offered for sale by private families is often a good buy. While the quality is easier to evaluate than that of appliances, the markdown is surprisingly generous. However, prices are even less consistent than those found in the used appliance field.

In general, few serviceable rugs, draperies, curtains, and other textile furnishings can be found in the used market. Certain antique oriental rugs are exceptions to this rule, but they clearly do not fall within the "economy" class. However, it is sometimes possible to salvage good sections from the border areas of a rug that shows wear only in the center where the normal traffic patterns occur. If wide enough, the border areas can serve as hall runners. Check department store sales for irregulars, close-outs, and regular stock reductions when looking for draperies and bedspreads. Many stores offer custom-made draperies at a worthwhile savings once or twice a year. Ask the drapery department manager for information.

While it is important to balance skills with your personal need for perfection, with even minimum sewing skills you can cut drapery and textile accessory costs. While major reupholstering may intimidate the non-professional, you could investigate some less ambitious projects. Draperies, floor and sofa pillow covers, table linens, simple casement curtains, decorative hangings, quilts, and bedspreads require less fitting. You will find that some upholstering is quick, easy, and highly rewarding in both money and satisfaction. You might like to experiment with slip seats on dining room chairs, padded cornices and headboards, and removable cushions on chairs. To help you get started, you might consult a good sewing reference book; however, when replacing an existing cover, following the original pattern and procedures is often sufficient guidance.

Used mattresses and springs are readily available, especially in salvage shops. However, such items are somewhat risky and fumigation is a necessary safeguard. In general, the springs tend to sag, padding is worn, and little life remains. Perhaps a better choice for temporary use might be a new foam pad laid on a solid board or door. When the budget allows a new mattress and springs, the pad and support could serve in other situations.

On the whole, shopping for used home furnishings can be fun and financially rewarding, if you have sufficient time and are willing to wait until a suitable buy can be found. While little technical ability is required to select comfortable, well constructed furniture or accessories for the home, certain repair skills are helpful. To guide the beginner and provide some new techniques for the more skilled, several references on reupholstering and refinishing have been included at the end of this book.

When looking for used furniture and accessories, investigate secondhand and antique shops, sales from model homes or apartments, auctions, swap shops, salvage stores, and rummage and garage sales. Search the classified advertising section of your newspaper or, in some cities, flyers listing goods offered by private owners that are distributed free in shopping centers. Community bulletin boards may also be available. Once or twice a year, household movers auction goods left unclaimed in their storage warehouses. While these sales are advertised in the newspaper, a telephone call could provide advance notice. Farm or garage sales, bazaars given by service organizations, churches, and even personal friends are other sources to investigate when looking for used home furnishings.

If decorative panels or other architectural ornaments interest you, it is possible to salvage some pieces when older buildings are demolished.

In many instances, unfortunately, a secondhand shop will handle the salvage operation directly, reselling at full market value. However, sometimes an absolutely free visit to the city dump may reward the diligent with similar ornaments, and in some cases, surprisingly serviceable furniture.

Trade-in, rental, and surplus furnishings are also available to a lesser extent. A few furniture retail outlets accept trade-ins, but less frequently than in the past. A more recent development, residential furniture rental stores, can be found in many cities. Often all or part of the rental payments are deductible if the furniture is purchased later. When considering such an arrangement, it is important to check comparable prices for similar furnishings at conventional retail outlets. Next, read the rental contract thoroughly, noting the mandatory rental period before possible purchase and any carrying charges or cleaning and damage deposits. Generally speaking, this is an expensive method.

Furniture and department stores have home furnishings sales several times a year, usually during February and August. Goods offered may be regularly stocked items or special purchases. Before buying any soiled or slightly damaged furniture, weigh the necessary renovation and cleaning as this cost can lower or completely cancel the initial savings.

Before shopping for used furniture, compare prices of suitable new pieces at several stores. Investigate the unfinished furniture offerings too, adding the cost of needed supplies and tools to the total price. The greater your knowledge of the furniture market, the more you are likely to select wisely.

## FURNITURE

Selection of furniture for the home should be based on knowledge of basic materials, construction methods, and general design factors. When evaluating used furniture, the points of greatest wear should be checked to determine whether repairs will be needed.

### Wood

Both hard and soft woods, used separately or in combination, are found in furniture. The softwoods, such as redwood, pine, and cedar, are more frequently selected for ready-to-finish and outdoor furniture. Such woods are less expensive, lack the distinctive grain, and are less durable than the hardwood group. The hardwoods, such as maple, cherry, birch, walnut, oak, or African mahogany, are commonly used in fine quality furniture. The grain markings are more distinctive and the natural wood tones warmer, showing greater depth than the soft group. While hardwood takes a finer finish, great smoothness and distinctive grain may be wasted in certain cases, such as outdoor furniture or furniture finished with opaque paints where the grain is completely hidden. Hardwoods are also selected where greater serviceability is required, such as in drawer runners or table tops.

Wood can be used in furniture either in solid form or layered construction. When solid wood has been used, the surface can be planed in case of damage, or thoroughly sanded and refinished. However, the tendency for wood to warp, shrink, or swell is greater in solid than in layered construction. Veneers, plywood, or laminated wood are all layered processes. Plywood and veneers consist of an odd number of layers glued together with the grain of successive layers arranged at right angles for greater strength, as shown in Figure 8–1.

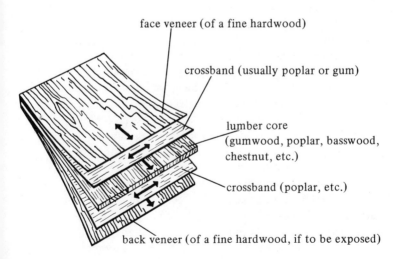

face veneer (of a fine hardwood)

crossband (usually poplar or gum)

lumber core
(gumwood, poplar, basswood, chestnut, etc.)

crossband (poplar, etc.)

back veneer (of a fine hardwood, if to be exposed)

Figure 8–1 *Typical veneer construction*

Veneering is not a new technique, but was known in ancient Greece and Rome. It was revived during the 1800s by the great cabinetmakers; however, modern adhesives gave veneer its durability and resistance to moisture and heat.

*Joint construction.* Wood can be joined in a number of different ways, some superior in strength to others. Regardless of the joining method, all members need to be glued for strength. While earlier vegetable or casein-based glues were loosened by heat, moisture, or age, the new adhesives are far more durable.

Of the joint constructions shown in Figure 8–2, the dovetail is the strongest. When buying a chest, the most durable drawers are dovetailed to better resist the normal strain at this point. The mortise and tenon joint is stronger than dowel construction. However, both methods are superior to the butt joining. This is the weakest joint of all and, unless strengthened with a corner block, should be avoided in furniture construction. You will also find corner blocks, notched and screwed in place, wherever extra rigidity is desirable as in chair, sofa, and table leg construction where strain is the greatest.

*Finish.* A great variety of finishes are used on furniture (see Table 8–1, p. 140). Finishes may penetrate the wood or remain on the surface; some are opaque, others transparent. Sometimes an older piece of furniture can be given new distinction by removing a heavy opaque layer of paint and replacing it with a transparent preservative that exposes the beauty of original grain markings. In other instances, where there are many scars and imperfections, or base material is nondescript; a bright coat of paint may be just what is needed.

Often old furniture needs only a thorough cleaning rather than refinishing. Neglect and many years' accumulation of grime dulls any finish, making it unattractive. To see if a surface can be rejuvenated without complete stripping, check for any brittleness or lack of adhesion in the present finish. Scratch an inconspicuous surface with the edge of a coin. If you do not scrape through easily to the base wood, the old finish is in fairly good shape and probably can be cleaned and given new life without the lengthy process of refinishing, unless scars or stains are present.

Dovetail joint

Mortise and tenon

Double dowel joining

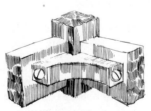

Corner block

Butt joint

**Figure 8−2** *Commonly used joining techniques for furniture construction*

**TABLE 8–1**
*Common wood finishes*

| Name | Results |
| --- | --- |
| Enamel | Generally hard and durable. May be glossy or dull. Rubbing with pumice and oil imparts a satin-like surface. Wide range of colors. |
| Lacquer | Harder than paints and varnishes and more resistant to heat and stains. Generally sprayed, as it dries rapidly. |
| Oil | Penetrating, durable finish with soft luster. Protective but not conspicuous; darkens and yellows wood to a degree. Must be renewed. Modern resin-oil finishes require less hand rubbing than older linseed oil-turpentine method. |
| Shellac | Fairly fragile finish affected by heat and moisture. Changes appearance of wood only slightly. Synthetic varnishes and penetrating wood sealers have largely replaced shellac. |
| Stain | Changes color of wood without covering grain, often emphasizing grain lines; usually darkens wood. |
| Synthetics | Many impregnating finishes with excellent moisture-resisting qualities; durable. |
| Varnish | Thin durable surface coating with little penetration; ranges from dull to high gloss. Probably the easiest finish coat for the do-it-yourself worker but best when not applied thickly, or resulting finish may be gummy. |
| Wax | Paste wax applied over a completely smooth surface previously sealed with a coat of shellac or varnish, thoroughly dried, imparts a pleasing, mellow luster. Wax penetrates raw wood and is impossible to remove thoroughly unless applied over sealing finish should refinishing eventually be desired. |

*Common points of wear.* In addition to evaluating wood selection, method of joining, and soundness of finish, inspect the usual areas of wear or damage when considering a used item.

*Table, desk, chest tops.* These may be of wood, plastic, linoleum, vinyl, cork, glass, or stone, such as marble and slate. All materials have inherent advantages and problems, but of all surfaces, wood is probably easiest to repair and refinish. With the possible exception or cork, replacement is often the only satisfactory solution when working with other materials. Any table, desk, or chest top receives considerable wear and frequently shows scratches, stains, bruises, small holes, or dents after years of use. Warping is more prevalent in solid than veneer construction. And while a faint warp perhaps adds charm to an antique table, the problem becomes less amusing when the table lacks this venerable quality. When a center leaf has been stored on end, it often warps. Pull apart any table with a center leaf, inserting the extension and checking the fit.

*Table edges and ornamentation.* These surfaces are easily nicked through use. If the scar is slight and there are no missing sections of ornament, perhaps one of the easier finish repair techniques suggested in Chapter Nine may be satisfactory. When ornamental trim has been partially destroyed, complete removal of the remaining section may often modernize furniture lines. In other instances, replacement or reconstruction may be desired. Many hardware stores and lumber yards carry a variety of easy-to-apply wood or synthetic ornamental moldings.

*Drawers.* Remove all drawers in any storage furniture, checking the runners for signs of wear or cracking. If worn, replace runners with hardwood strips, or in some instances, a putty-type epoxy can be used to build up slightly worn runners. For greater sliding ease, wax or a thin flexible nylon stripping can be applied. Very heavy drawers or sliding shelves move easiest when suspended on nylon-type rollers or tracks found in many hardware, lumber, or builders' supply stores.

*Handles, knobs, and hinges.* All should be securely attached to a wood surface with screws rather than nails. A loose-fitting knob or handle indicates worn threads in the adjacent wood member. Rebuilding is not impossible, but takes some time. While a missing drawer pull can be difficult to find in a matching pattern, sometimes replacement with a completely new set of attractive hardware adds distinction to an older piece.

*Furniture legs and bases.* Test furniture on a level floor by rocking gently to check balance. Strangely enough, one leg often wears shorter than the others over a period of time. A wobbly table or chair continually irritates the user if not repaired. Legs and bases of furniture suffer abrasion from users' shoes and vacuum cleaners pushed carelessly, or without proper furniture guards.

*Joint construction.* Gently rock the frame of any cabinet, chest, sofa, or chair to check for looseness in joint areas. If this is a problem, the joined areas probably need regluing, replacement of corner blocks, or new screws. Check for cracks as well.

**Metal or Plastic**

While metal furniture generally has been reserved for outdoor use in the past, today many pieces are appearing inside the home as well. Metal, glass, tile, and laminated plastic table surfaces are easy to clean and resist stains better than wood. Since metal is so strong, it can take many forms in furniture. We find it used in free-form chairs as steel wire mesh, inspired by Harry Bertoia; in heavy cast shapes for patio or garden use; or in lightweight tubular aluminum form for easy portability. While the basic material is strong, needed repairs usually pose more problems for an average owner than with wood. Variety exists in colors and finishes as well. To name just a few, a wide range of enamel hues are applied to steel; aluminum can be anodized for a colored or frosty appearance; and chromium plating, frequently used in contemporary chairs and tables, can be obtained in a wide range of finishes.

Metal frames are often used with other materials. The typical kitchen table and chairs with chrome-plated steel frames, laminated plastic table top, and vinyl seats has been popular for many years. We also find molded, glass-reinforced polyester, contoured to fit the body with or without further cushioning, resting on metal supports; tubular aluminum or steel chairs and lounges with saran straps, vinyl, leather, or more conventional fabric cushions. Metal appears in table constructions as well. We find a variety sold for outdoor use, but elegant coffee tables of glass and chrome-plated steel can also be found.

Metal can be fabricated in a variety of ways, each with a characteristic appearance and strength. Welding provides the smoothest and strongest connection and is used most frequently in finer quality furniture. Other pieces are joined by riveting or bolting. A very handsome yet inexpensive desk can be made from a narrow door supported by a frame of surplus aluminum angle strips bolted together at the ends. The visible manner of joining will seem compatible with the materials selected.

Plastic in its many forms can be exciting as a furniture medium, lending itself both to rigid structures and to soft inflatables that move with the body. In most instances the used market offers less desirable plastic furniture than wood. The one possible exception may be the standard chrome and plastic kitchen table and chair set. Quite a few are offered by private sellers and salvage shops at low prices. However, plastic upholstery will usually need replacement. Repairing or refinishing plastic is difficult at best. While the used market fails to offer an abundance of low cost plastic furnishings, the new market provides a variety of inexpensive alternatives. Especially interesting visually are the colorful and sometimes comfortable inflatable plastic chairs and floor pillows.

## Other Materials

Other inexpensive furniture is made completely or partially of rattan, reed, or canvas. While these are less available in the used market, the initial new cost is relatively low compared with more conventional furnishings. If such furniture is purchased for temporary use in a home when a furnishings budget is low, it can still be useful in a patio or family room when a larger budget makes more permanent furniture possible. In the meantime, it offers comfortable, attractive seating at an economical price.

## Upholstered Furniture

The quality of any upholstered furniture is difficult to judge. The inner construction, whether in new or secondhand chairs or sofas, is often much of a mystery to the average consumer. When buying new upholstered furniture, we often rely on a salesman's advice or the dependability of a manufacturer's name. In the used market, the brand name may offer some guidance but sales advice is often unreliable. When shopping for a used sofa or chair, the best index of condition is probably comfort. Test a chair or sofa by sitting, trying all the normal positions you take when relaxing, reading, or conversing. If comfortable, the piece is worth further investigation.

*Springs and stuffing.* Sagging springs are fairly obvious to the buyer, as is worn padding or foam cushions that have lost their resiliency and are beginning to crumble. Check the underside of upholstered pieces for signs of wear. While you can replace foam or polyester padding, retie springs, and change webbing, it is to be hoped that such problems will come as no surprise after a purchase. If coiled springs have been used, they should be tied closely enough both to the webbing and the frame to prevent sagging. In slimmer, more contemporary furniture construction, foam padding is often placed over flat thin springs, webbing, or directly on a wood frame.

Older upholstery stuffing included hair, down, kapok cotton, and even moss, all of which were fairly undesirable from a sanitation as well as a practical standpoint. More recently, foam padding has become fairly standard in upholstery construction. It is often covered with polyester fiberfill for added comfort and shape. Unlike earlier stuffings, both materials are resistant to moths and other insects. Molded foam is considered more desirable in upholstery construction than shredded for purposes of comfort and durability.

*Upholstery fabric.* Whether evaluating the durability of existing upholstery coverings before purchasing or selecting replacement upholstery, a knowledge of the fiber characteristics shown in Table 8—2 will help. However, in addition to fiber composition, weave structure must be considered when evaluating the wear potential of any upholstery fabric. A balanced construction in which yarns of similar size and twist are woven in a firm twill or plain weave offers the greatest stability and resistance to wear. Unbalanced satin and damask weaves, thick and thin constructions where a fine warp supports heavier filling yarns, and irregular or loosely woven fabrics are all more susceptible to abrasion than the balanced weaves.

Most frequently, upholstery fabric is selected for esthetic reasons alone. While few would argue that beauty is important, fabric that does not clean or resist abrasion loses its attractiveness within a few months, especially in the presence of several active youngsters. Appearance is important, but the practical aspects of potential wear and maintenance should be considered to insure long-range consumer satisfaction.

**TABLE 8–2**
*Textile fiber characteristics summary*

| Fiber | Home Furnishings Uses | Characteristics | Maintenance |
| --- | --- | --- | --- |
| Acetate | Bedspreads, curtains, draperies, upholstery | Poor resistance to abrasion, sunlight. Hangs well. | Dry-clean or wash as directed. Iron at cool temperature. |
| Acrylic | Blankets, carpets, upholstery, curtains, table linens | Subject to static electricity. Resistant to sun degradation and wrinkling. | Easy to spot-clean, dry-clean or wash as instructed; dries quickly. Remove oily stains before washing. |
| Cotton | All household textiles | Poor wrinkle and shrink resistance unless treated. Blends well with other fibers. Medium resistance to abrasion and sunlight. | Dry-clean or wash as directed; irons easily. Protect against mildew. |
| Glass | Curtains, draperies | Fireproof and resistant to moisture and salt air. Poor abrasion and flexing resistance, although newer processes have increased flexibility. | Easy soil removal; hand wash; do not iron. Dries quickly. |

**TABLE 8–2** (Cont'd)

| Fiber | Home Furnishings Uses | Characteristics | Maintenance |
|---|---|---|---|
| Linen | Curtains, draperies, upholstery, rugs, household linens | Wrinkles easily unless treated. Shrinks unless Sanforized. Medium abrasion and sunlight resistance. | Washes and irons well at high temperature; protect from moisture to prevent mildew. |
| Moda-crylic | Rugs, upholstery | Resistant to fire; self-extinguishing. Good resistance to abrasion and sunlight. | Easy to launder; dries quickly; iron at extremely low temperatures only. |
| Nylon | Bedspreads, rugs, upholstery, draperies, curtains | Good draping quality. Outstanding elasticity, strength, resistance to abrasion and wrinkling. Subject to static electricity. | Washes easily but tends to attract soil. Remove oily stains before laundering. Iron at low temperature. |
| Olefin | Blankets, rugs, upholstery, webbing | No water absorption. Low melting temperature. Good resistance to abrasion, wrinkling, and sunlight. | Spot-clean or wash. |
| Polyester | Bedding, curtains, draperies, upholstery, rugs and fiberfill | Exceptional resistance to wrinkling. Often appears in blends. Good resistance to abrasion and sunlight. | Dry-clean or wash as directed; dries quickly; requires little ironing. Remove oily stains before washing. |

| Fiber | Home Furnishings Uses | Characteristics | Maintenance |
|-------|----------------------|-----------------|-------------|
| Rayon | All general household textiles | Moderately durable. Lacks resiliency; wrinkles easily. Moderate resistance to abrasion and sunlight. | Dry-clean or wash as directed. May shrink or stretch if not treated for resistance. |
| Saran | Upholstery and webbing | Resists soils, stains and weathering. Melts at low heat. Moderate resistance to abrasion and sunlight. Dimensionally stable. | Spot-clean, sponge, or wash; dries quickly. |
| Silk | Draperies, rugs, upholstery | Poor resistance to sunlight. Moderate resistance to abrasion and wrinkling. | Dry-clean or hand wash; iron at moderate temperature. |
| Wool | Blankets, draperies, rugs, upholstery | Excellent resiliency. Moderate resistance to abrasion, sunlight. Blends well with other fibers. | Spot-clean, dry-clean, or wash in cold water unless specially treated to retard shrinking. |

### When Is Furniture Restoration Worthwhile?

Furniture does not have to fall within the antique category to merit restoration, but it should have charm and be appropriate to your home to justify the time and labor required. Before buying, ask yourself:

Is it functional for my purpose and will it fit within the space available in my home? (Consider the scale of other furnishings as well.)

Do the lines and proportions please me? Does it contribute to the
  character I want to achieve in my home?

Is the condition of wood, color, and grain pleasing to my eye; can it
  be changed accordingly?

Are parts missing and, if so, what are the possibilities of replacement;
  what tools and materials will be required; what skill is needed for
  such replacement?

Can a new piece be found for nearly the same price that will solve my
  problem as well?

What is the nature of repair and renovation required to make this piece
  of furniture suitable for my home; do I have the necessary skill
  and patience for the job?


## FLOOR AND WINDOW COVERINGS

Quality in both is difficult to find when shopping in the used market.
However, good buys can be found in department stores during regularly
scheduled home furnishings sales. Secondhand area rugs are offered
by private sellers in the newspaper classified ads and by salvage shops.
The quality of those offered by private sellers is superior to other
outlets with the exception of authentic oriental rugs, which fall in the
collector's classification and are sold through special outlets and priced
accordingly. Auctions sometimes provide surprisingly good buys in
both general and rare floor coverings, although many worn examples
are sold as well.

Consider fiber characteristics before selecting either floor or window
coverings, paying special attention to sunlight resistance. Construction
in floor or window coverings is as important a consideration as it is
in upholstery selection. While a firm balanced weave structure is
important in both upholstery and drapery selection, rugs also benefit
from a firm construction. When selecting a pile rug, density is of
primary importance. The more tufts per square inch, the greater the
durability. Next, check the backing for flexibility and strength.
Extremely long shag construction, while often in fashion, is difficult
if not impossible to clean thoroughly and maintain. Pennock and
Jaeger reported a 14-year life expectancy for living room wool rugs or

carpeting, a figure which seems valid today.[2]  A pad under any rug
will add to its life span and should be considered a necessity when
purchasing any good soft floor covering.

While draperies and curtains are almost nonexistent in the secondhand
market, inexpensive blinds can at times be found through salvage outlets,
although they will frequently need some repairs.  Special sales and do-it-
yourself window coverings seem the best answer for the budget-minded
consumer.

## ACCESSORIES

Accessories are the finishing touches in your home and express your
family interests, tastes, and ideas.  They include things we hang on walls,
certain useful objects — such as wastebaskets and ashtrays — as well as
the purely decorative objects that generally serve only esthetic purposes.

### Wall Hangings

These include pictures, mirrors, shelves, collages, clocks, and textiles.
The possibilities are endless although the selection is more or less
dependent upon room size, furnishings budget, and personal taste.
To add warmth to a sparsely furnished room, attractive rugs can be
hung on a wall, lending their own unique color and texture.  A large
section of attractive fabric can be stapled over a canvas stretcher
(available in artist supply shops) and hung as a picture, or a length may
be hemmed and supported by a dowel rod serving as a room divider.

Maps, posters, and museum reproductions of original paintings are
attractive, and if you frame them yourself they are inexpensive hangings.  Check for frames in secondhand or salvage stores.  An attractive
frame can also be used to mount a mirror for your bedroom, hall, or
bath with style at less cost than you will pay in a regular retail outlet.

### Useful Objects

Some can be constructed at almost no cost.  Make wastebaskets using
large ice cream containers.  Paint or cover with contact paper or

[2] Jean L. Pennock, Carol M. Jaeger, "Household Service Life of Durable Goods,"
*Journal of Home Economics* (January, 1964), p. 23.

fabric and trim. A well-scrubbed, unadorned clay flower pot makes an attractive and highly suitable container for a large fern.

Books and magazines add splashes of color and warmth when arranged on shelves, racks, or tables. While books may be considered useful but decorative accessories, we do not purchase them in quite the same manner as if we were choosing a vase or wall hanging. Regardless, secondhand shops are good places to look for books. Whether seeking older books with an eye toward those of potential value to collectors or simply selecting good reading at a small price, you will often be rewarded. One buyer purchased a hundred-year-old encyclopedia, paying 25 cents a pound — a somewhat curious method of evaluating the worth of a book.

Many useful accessories, such as serving trays, bookends, baskets, quilts, and lamps, can be found in secondhand or salvage shops and at auctions. Often the lamps are rather tiny, non-functional in design, and generally inadequate fixtures. However, new shades and hardware or entire lamp kits can be purchased in the electrical department of any large hardware store if the original purchase merits. Examine pole lamps for missing parts as the center spring section falls out easily.

## Decorative Objects

These are chosen simply for beauty or sentimental value. Important purchases should be made with care, but in the meantime, inexpensive ornaments such as bowls of fruit, nuts, pine cones, Christmas balls, candles, do-it-yourself craft projects, or even a basket of needlework and yarn adds color to a room and personalizes the area in a meaningful way. The possibilities are unlimited.

# 9

# furniture repairs, maintenance, and cleaning

In many instances, damaged furniture surfaces can be repaired without a complete refinishing or expensive tools and supplies. Often, supplies already on hand are sufficient to restore scratched or neglected surfaces. Many charming older pieces of furniture need only a thorough cleaning and polishing to become attractive assets to your home. In our enthusiasm we sometimes suffer from the desire to over-restore furniture, losing much of the original charm in the process. Remember that antiques are valued because of their age. And although we hope our older furniture carries those years gracefully, a bruise or stain in an otherwise well built "collectable" may lend a certain charm.

When surface damage is not excessive, dents and scratches in wood can often be repaired without removing the original finish beyond the surface wax layer. Metals and plastics are more difficult to repair and often require new parts rather than simple refinishing. A variety of techniques are suggested for blemish removal on wood surfaces, but it is always best to test first in an inconspicuous spot. With the variety of woods and finishes available today, it takes practice to select the best method of removing any blemish. Several alternative procedures are given in this chapter when choices are available.

Cleaning and general care suggestions are also offered below that will protect and enhance the beauty of much of the furniture found in the home. Some understanding of wood finishing techniques is vital if we are to select proper cleaners and waxes from the countless varieties available. The more costly products are not always the best for protection and cleaning. And though wax enhances many finishes, a heavy build-up will dull the original beauty of any piece.

Secondhand upholstered furniture is usually in need of a thorough cleaning at the time of purchase. When buying an exceptionally fine piece with delicate upholstery (or heavily soiled furniture), a professional cleaning may be needed; in other instances, inexpensive home shampooing may suffice. While many commerical shampoos are available, an inexpensive solution of detergent and water is equally successful in most situations. Regardless of the cleaner selected, test on a hidden fabric surface before using in order to avoid any possible fading or other damage to the upholstery. We have suggested some stain removal techniques to handle common home accidents. Remember, old stains are more difficult to remove than fresh ones and there is always less possibility of complete removal after any stain has dried. With severely stained upholstered furniture, reupholstering or slip-covering may be the only answer.

## WOOD SURFACES

A thorough cleaning and conditioning of older wood surfaces may restore the original beauty in many pieces of furniture. Others with scratches, dents, or bruises will need further work to repair the damages of age and abuse. When the surface is severely damaged, complete refinishing and repair is the only satisfactory answer.

### Regular Cleaning and Polishing

Varnish, shellac, oil, penetrating wood sealer, lacquer, wax, and paint are all used in finishing furniture. However, countless variations exist in the composition and application of these basic finishes. For example, paint may have either a high gloss or matte finish. It may be applied "as is," antiqued, spattered, stippled, marbleized, distressed, or highlighted with gold. Synthetic finishes have eased application greatly and added a resistance to many stains not possible in the earlier compounds. Most varnishes today are made from synthetic resins; other clear plastic-based finishes such as the polyurethanes offer even greater resistance to abrasion, water, and oil stains.

For care and cleaning purposes, all of these finishes fall into five general classifications:

*High gloss finishes.* For best results, protect with a paste wax or liquid polish. When using a paste wax, apply thinly, buffing to a high sheen. Heavy coats of wax become gummy, collect dirt, and obscure the original wood finish. Liquid polishes, which require less rubbing, should be poured onto a soft cloth for application and never directly onto the furniture surface. Buff thoroughly, using a clean cloth until the surface is dry and hard. If not completely buffed, the residue will attract dust.

*Satin gloss finishes.* To preserve the finish, protect with a cleaning polish or cream wax that does not contain silicone. This additive will increase the sheen, destroying the desired satin finish. However, even with the proper polish or wax, the resulting gloss normally heightens after a number of applications. When this effect becomes noticeable, it is time to completely remove the built-up wax and start anew.

*Low gloss finishes.* Select a low luster polish or cleaning wax designed to clean and protect the finish without adding unwanted luster. Apply the polish or wax sparingly between two layers of cloth to ensure that only a thin layer coats the wood surface. For best results, wax small areas at a time, immediately buffing until the finish is hard and dry. A waxed surface which is insufficiently buffed will collect dust.

*Penetrating oil finishes.* Traditionally, linseed oil was used to preserve and beautify many woods. More recently, penetrating resin-oil finishes have been developed which require fewer hours of hand rubbing than the original finish and yet impart the same natural beauty. As a bonus, newer finishes withstand stains and water remarkably well.

The boiled linseed or resin-oil finishes need only occasional washing and cleaning with mineral spirits followed by the original oil. To apply the oil, use a large pad of soft cloth, rubbing vigorously with the grain. When finished, wipe away all excess. To avoid the possibility of spontaneous combustion, thoroughly wash or destroy oily rags IMMEDIATELY after the treatment.

Oiled finishes should never be waxed as the two materials are not compatible. However, if wax has been applied inadvertently, remove thoroughly with mineral spirits before reapplying the original oil. To remove scratches or blemishes, rub lightly with the grain with very fine steel wool. Wash and allow to air dry. Next wipe with mineral spirits and re-oil, using the original finish preparation.

*Paint finishes.* Though the variety of paint finishes found on furniture is almost endless, most are easy to maintain by washing with mild suds and water. Use water sparingly, especially around the joints, but rinse thoroughly to remove any soap residue as it will dull the finish. Dry quickly to preserve both wood and glue. When protecting furniture with wax or liquid polish, select a type suitable for painted finishes.

### Special Cleaning and Conditioning

A thorough washing once or twice a year will remove much of the soil, wax, and other residue that collects on wood surfaces. Work on small areas at a time so that the surface does not remain wet longer than necessary. Take special care when washing near joints fastened with older water-soluble glues: older glues are far less resistant to moisture and pose greater problems than modern adhesives. To wash, use a mild sudsy solution, cleaning with a soft cloth from which most of the water has been wrung. Rinse thoroughly and wipe dry immediately with a clean cloth. When the accumulation of dirt is heavy, more than one washing may be needed. If a wax residue remains after washing, use a commercial wax remover, mineral spirits, or an oil-based turpentine to remove stubborn traces. All are available at most hardware and paint stores.

A furniture cleaner-conditioner can be substituted for soap and water when removing built-up dirt, smoke, and wax. This is often the wiser choice when in doubt about the water resistance of older adhesives. Commercial preparations are available or, if you prefer, make your own cleaner-conditioner quite inexpensively. Combine three parts boiled linseed oil and one part gum turpentine in a tightly covered container; shake well. (Be sure to use only commercially prepared boiled linseed oil.) Float a small amount of this solution over the surface of hot water in a container. Dip a soft cloth into the oily solution, rubbing briskly over a small area at a time. Wring out a clean cloth in clear warm water and rinse the surface. Wipe completely dry with a third soft cloth.

When cleaning difficult areas such as carvings or moldings, apply the cleaner-conditioner with a stiff brush or a wooden toothpick tipped with cotton. If the initial cleaning is incomplete, dip a fine 3/0 steel wool pad into the cleaner-conditioner and rub lightly in the grain direction to remove embedded soil. IMPORTANT: Do not reheat water with cleaner as it is highly inflammable. When cool, throw away and start anew.

## Repairs

While scars may be such that complete refinishing of a wood surface is necessary, in other instances minor repairs involving considerably less effort may substantially improve the appearance. When structural repairs are needed, such as the regluing of joints or replacement of a broken member, either seek expert advice or consult one of the many references available that offer the necessary detailed instructions. A number of these manuals have been listed in the reference section of this book. However, your state Cooperative Extension Service and the U.S. Department of Agriculture publish many bulletins explaining these repairs in detail. All are free or available at nominal prices.

*Bruises and dents.* Moderate depressions in furniture surfaces can be raised with the application of water or, in some instances, water and heat. Hard maple is the one exception to the rule and nothing, short of sanding and refinishing, corrects the problem.

*Softwoods.* When removing a dent from pine, cedar, or other softwood furniture surface, fill the depression with water. Allow the wood to absorb the water, adding more as needed until the surface has risen a bit higher than the surrounding wood area. To speed this process, you may pierce the bruised surface in several spots with a fine needle. (These holes will be invisible when the repair is completed.) When dry, the swollen area should shrink to the original level without further treatment.

*Hardwoods.* The hardwoods such as birch, oak, teak, and walnut are more resistant to moisture and require the addition of heat to correct any dents or bruises. Fill the depressed area with water as described above. Heat may be added in several ways: some use a steam iron, lightly touching a damp cloth laid over the bruised area; others heat a metal object such as an old screwdriver blade, placing it in the water until steam forms. Care is needed to avoid touching the wood surface itself — it will burn. When using this method, select a nearly worthless tool because heat destroys its original temper.

Both treatments are likely to leave cloudy white spots when applied to most wood finishes. Should this occur, follow the directions for removal of white spots given later in this chapter.

*Scratches and blemishes.* When wood furniture accumulates the scratches and blemishes that come with long or sometimes careless use, complete refinishing may be the only satisfactory repair. However, if the surface damage is not extensive, these flaws can in many instances be covered or removed completely without stripping the old finish. But it is necessary to remove all traces of wax from the damaged area before repair begins or the surface will not absorb the treatment. It is often preferable to remove all wax at this time to eliminate spotting the finish.

Furniture refinishing authorities offer many ways to lessen or remove scars. However, it is always wise to experiment first on an inconspicuous spot, as the original wood, finish, and blemish itself create a series of variables that must be considered when selecting an appropriate repair process. We have chosen the most common blemish removal recipes offered for home use. All have been tested on wood surfaces with good results and require only readily available supplies plus a minimum of skill.

When treating minor scratches and blemishes, several treatments seem to work well:

*Nutmeats or linseed oil.* Both provide enough coloring to hide minor scratches. Break a shelled nut in half and rub the broken surface well into the scratch. Brazil nuts and black walnuts are both especially effective for stain removal. If you prefer, linseed oil can be applied in the same way. Rub briskly with your finger to cover all scratched areas. You will be amazed at the results.

*Crayon.* Select one that comes closest to the color of the finish. Fill scratches with the crayon wax, rubbing in well with your finger. Should the color selected be too dark, remove with mineral spirits. Wipe with a soft dry cloth and rewax. If you prefer, wax-sticks which are somewhat softer than ordinary crayons can be purchased in paint stores. These are made especially for repairing scratches and are available in a variety of wood tones.

*Shoe polish.* Use a paste wax nearest the color of the original finish to hide scratches. Brown blends well with walnut finishes; cordovan with mahogany; light tan for blond woods; and black for lacquered finishes. Apply polish with a cotton-tipped stick or your finger, rubbing well into the blemish. Next, buff with a soft cloth until dry.

*Rottenstone and oil.* A more abrasive treatment than those previously suggested may be more effective when encountering a stubborn scratch. Rottenstone, a finer abrasive than pumice, is available in paint or hardware stores. To repair scratches, coat damaged surface with a few drops of salad oil; add enough rottenstone to make a paste and then, using a soft cloth, rub scratched area working with the grain. Wipe frequently with a clean cloth and a few drops of salad oil to compare and match the original surface.

To repair deeper scratches or blemishes, the surface requires building as well as re-staining. In these cases, repair is somewhat more time consuming and demands greater patience.

*Oil stain and shellac.* Dilute a scant spoonful of oil stain with a few drops of naphtha or turpentine. A matching oil rather than spirit-based stain should be used to avoid damaging the existing finish. Apply the diluted stain with a small brush or cotton-tipped toothpick, working until the scratched surface matches the color of the adjacent finish. Let the stain dry for 12 hours.

Next, build up the damaged area, using either a liquid shellac or special filling sticks that are softened with heat. These sticks are available in paint stores in a variety of wood tones. When using liquid shellac, apply and let dry for at least four hours. Repeat the process as many times as necessary to build up the scratched area, drying carefully between each coat.

To finish, sand the repaired area with 8/0 sandpaper, rubbing very lightly with the grain of the wood until even with surrounding surface. Follow sanding with rottenstone and oil treatment as described earlier. When the surface is dry, rewax and buff.

White spots are very common furniture blemishes caused by heat and/or moisture. The ease of removal depends upon the depth of damage and the original finish. In some cases, completely removing the wax layer will also remove the blemish. In other instances, more extensive repairs are required. The following remedies have been most succesful in treating these troublesome furniture stains for many years:

*Cigar or cigarette ashes.* Ashes are a mild alkaline abrasive that cannot damage a finish and yet are often successful in removing cloudy white blemishes when the damage is not too extensive. To apply, briskly rub ashes into the white area using a soft cloth lightly moistened with salad or sewing machine oil. Periodically wipe off the area and inspect. If the treatment results in complete removal, wipe, let dry and rewax. For somewhat greater abrasion, rottenstone or ordinary table salt may be used in the same manner.

*3/F pumice and linseed oil.* For stubborn cases where deeper damage has occurred, use pumice and linseed oil in the manner described above. To wipe off the surface for comparison, rub with the grain using a cloth moistened slightly with naphtha.

*Ammonia.* When white spots remain on a varnished surface, household ammonia often brings results. To apply, first wring out a soft cloth in clear water, then apply a few drops of ammonia. Rub the cloth over the spotted area lightly, polishing with a dry cloth. If removal is satisfactory, rewax and buff.

## OTHER SURFACES

Wood is used more frequently in furniture for the home than any other material. However, plastics, leather, marble, cane, and metal are also important in furniture design and a knowledge of their care is needed.

### Laminated Plastics

These hard-surfaced finishes promise maximum ease of care. They resist stains, scuffs, and heat remarkably well, requiring only soap and water cleaning. Laminated plastic surfaces are often found in children's rooms, kitchens, family rooms, baths, or in any situation where especially hard use is expected. Laminated plastic is tough but not indestructible. Protect surfaces from extreme heat and sharp knife blades. A counter *should not* be used as a chopping block. Wipe up spills immediately to avoid stains. (However, modern laminated plastics are quite resistant to staining.)

For greater protection and luster, consider a wax or polish designed specifically for plastics, since general purpose waxes made for wood surfaces often cause streaking. A worn surface can be revitalized to some extent with a single-step automobile cleaner-polish. To apply, pour the polish on a soft thick cloth and rub worn areas with firm lengthwise strokes until an even gloss develops. Wipe with a clean cloth, and when thoroughly dry, apply cream polish or silicone-based wax.

## Leather

To remove soil, wash occasionally using just the foam of a mild soap solution, wetting the surface as little as possible. Rinse several times using a clean damp cloth to remove all traces of soap. For protection and luster, follow with a layer of fine quality furniture cream. Saddle-soap or a special leather preservative can be used to keep the surfaces soft and supple. When leather appears dry, you might apply neat's-foot oil, castor oil, or a good leather conditioner.

Certain precautions are necessary when caring for leather to avoid damaging the surface. To prevent surface cracking, avoid silicone polishes, heavy paste, or liquid waxes. Mineral oil should also be avoided as it can soften and damage the surface. When glass is used to protect leather table tops, cushion first with felt bumpers at the corners to provide air circulation.

## Marble

Marble in its purest form is composed of carbonate of lime or limestone. It is porous, susceptible to stains, and can be dissolved in acid. When caring for marble surfaces, wash frequently using a soft cloth wrung out in a soap and water solution. Rinse carefully and wipe dry. Rinsing with a moderately wet cloth is especially important when cleaning, as dirty water can easily penetrate the porous finish, leaving permanent stains. Coasters are a must on marble table tops since even the moisture from a glass can cause a permanent stain.

Fruit juices, carbonated drinks, or other food acids should be wiped up immediately with a sudsy sponge to prevent surface etching. Acid cleaners also destroy the finish.

Hydrogen peroxide U.S.P. three per cent can be effective in removing many stains. Cover stained area and let set for several hours; rinse and dry. Treatment may be repeated if necessary. Commercial marble cleaner is also available, but *prevention* of stains is preferable because some do not respond to any treatment.

If marble becomes dull, add life with polishing putty or tin oxide; both are available in most hardware stores. To polish, sprinkle either lightly over the surface, rubbing briskly with a soft damp cloth until a shine appears. A colorless light paste wax can be applied to protect the surface; however, it may slightly yellow the appearance of white marble.

## Wicker

Wicker furniture is made from reed (cane), rattan (bamboo), or willow. Dust regularly with a vacuum cleaner dusting tool or soft brush, wiping up any spots with a damp cloth. At least once a year, wash thoroughly with suds and a garden hose to remove accumulated dust. In addition to cleaning, the hosing prevents these organic fibers from drying. Dry outdoors and repaint or varnish whenever necessary. Marine spar varnish is an excellent protective finish for both wicker furniture and baskets.

## Brass Fittings

Brass is commonly used in furniture fittings. When they are lacquered to resist tarnish they normally respond well to the same cleaning techniques used on the adjacent furniture surfaces. Otherwise, soap and water is your best cleaner.

When restoring furniture, remove unlacquered brass handles, keyhole plates, escutcheons, and hinges wherever possible. Polish with a commercial cleaner or household ammonia. To clean heavily encrusted solid brass hardware, use 3/0 steel wool and warm soapy water. Rinse and polish dry.

## Glass

Glass table tops can be kept clean with commercial cleaners or an inexpensive water and ammonia solution. Follow cleaning with wiping and polishing with a soft cloth until thoroughly dry and streak-free. When cleaning glass table tops or mirrors, take care not to wet adjacent wood or gilt surfaces that would be harmed by water or glass cleaner.

## Metal

Painted metal surfaces rarely need more than soap and water to retain their appearance. Steel or iron garden furniture may rust when the protective coating is damaged. Clean off rusted areas with a rust remover and refinish. Chrome, aluminum, and stainless steel furniture may all be washed with soap or detergent and water. Polish occasionally with metal cleaners or appliance wax. Aluminum garden furniture can be brightened with ordinary soap-filled steel wool pads and water whenever the surface becomes corroded from outdoor use.

## UPHOLSTERY

Ease of care depends mainly upon the choice of fabric. Many fabrics are available with soil resistant finishes, such as Scotchgard. While this process does not lend unlimited resistance, spills tend to "bead up" on the fabric surface, allowing easier immediate cleanup. If you are searching for a surface that is almost totally resistant to spills, look for a vinyl covering. To ensure satisfaction, select upholstery with your family and their habits in mind. The more fragile, hard-to-clean fabrics such as velvets and delicate silk brocades are generally more suitable to homes without active children or pets. In short, home upholstery cleaning and spotting is difficult at best!

### General Cleaning

To remove surface dust before it becomes imbedded grime, clean upholstery once a week either with vacuum cleaner attachments or a whisk broom, paying special attention to dirt-catching crevices. Remove any spots or stains while fresh with an appropriate cleaner. When spotting furniture with foam rubber padding, avoid dry-cleaning solvents which will cause eventual disintegration of the padding. When needed, use a foamy non-solvent based commercial shampoo or an inexpensive homemade detergent and water cleaner.

To prepare the homemade cleaner, whip 1/4 cup regular sudsing detergent into a quart of warm water, beating into a thick foam. Some homemakers add a tablespoon or two of ammonia to brighten a surface imbedded with greasy soil. Before shampooing, always vacuum thoroughly to remove surface dust. Then apply the "dry" foam with a sponge or brush, working in a circular motion, wetting only a small area at a time. Remove suds by wiping with a clean damp Turkish towel. Dry thoroughly in a well ventilated or heated room. Finally, vacuum again with the upholstery cleaning tool to remove any residue.

A word about slipcovers: when fabric coverings are removable for cleaning, so much the better. Even when a sofa or chair is upholstered rather than slipcovered, the cushions which receive the most wear should unzip for easy cleaning. Then, depending upon the fabric, they can be separately washed, dry-cleaned, or shampooed with upholstery cleaner.

While mild detergent or soap and water is all that is needed to keep vinyl upholstery spotless, once the surface becomes stained or dulled its restoration can be difficult. After washing, polish occasionally with a cream wax to help restore any lost luster. It is best to avoid harsh detergents when cleaning as they cause many vinyls to become brittle and eventually crack.

### Treatment of Common Stains

When treating stains, it is always best to test the remedy on an inconspicuous spot to check for possible damage. Removal of stains is always easier and more complete while they are fresh. As a general rule, avoid exposure to heat which tends to permanently set a good many stains. Actually, few stain removal supplies are required in the home, but it is well to store the common ones together for easy access when an emergency arises. Include a good stain removal chart (perhaps this book) for easy reference.

The commonly prescribed stain removal recipes given below are primarily of use in spot-treating upholstery. While the same cleaning agents are usually effective for treating draperies, rugs, table, or bed linens, the procedures may vary. As you might suspect, it is much easier to remove stains from readily launderable bed linens than from an upholstered chair.

*Alcoholic beverages.* Wipe up spilled drinks promptly and sponge fabrics with cool water to avoid permanent stains; however, when working on acetates, dilute one part alcohol with two parts water. Shampoo immediately after treating with water or alcohol.

*Blood.* When treating a washable fabric, soak in cold water until the stain is nearly gone, then wash as indicated using detergent and warm water. In treating stubborn stains, apply a paste of meat tenderizer and water to remove remaining traces. This is usually successful unless the bloodstain has been set with hot water. When working with non-washable fabrics or upholstered constructions, first sponge the stain with cold water, then shampoo with "dry" suds, rinsing with a damp cloth. If the stain is still visible, apply hydrogen peroxide to remove the final traces after first testing in an inconspicuous spot.

When removing blood from a rug, a paste made of an absorbent and cold water is very helpful in removing fresh stains. Cornstarch, talcum, or fuller's earth will serve well as the absorbent. Spread the paste thickly over the stained area, allowing it to dry. When dry, brush residue away and repeat the process until stain is completely removed.

*Candle wax.* Remove surface wax with dull knife. When the construction allows, place a towel under the stained surface and wet thoroughly several times with cleaning fluid. Dry and then launder washable fabrics. Should any dye remain, sponge the residue with a solution of one part alcohol and two parts water. When treating wall-to-wall carpeting or upholstery that does not lend itself to this method of removal, it is best to remove the surface wax and then seek the advice of a professional cleaner in removing the remaining stain.

*Chewing gum.* Harden the gum with an ice cube and then remove as much residue as possible with a dull knife. When possible soak the stained area with cleaning fluid and then launder or shampoo with upholstery cleaner. If you first harden gum to be removed from carpeting, you will often be able to rub all traces completely out of the pile without further treatment.

*Butter.* Laundering will remove the stain when treating washable fabrics; however, pretreating with detergent paste or a commercial spotting preparation may be necessary when treating polyester, nylon, and certain fiber blends. Sponge non-washables with cleaning fluid or use an absorbent such as talcum, fuller's earth, or cornstarch to remove oily stains. Shampoo with "dry" foam if any traces remain.

*Coffee and tea.* If no cream is involved, sponge with cool water or, when fiber and construction permit, soak for 30 minutes. Follow with laundering or shampooing. When cleaning upholstery, a final sponging with alcohol will speed the drying process. If cream was present in the spilled beverage, follow the above procedure with a final sponging using cleaning fluid to remove the greasy residue.

*Ballpoint pen ink.* Shampooing will remove some stains; others may respond to dry-cleaning solvent, slowly dripped through the spot. Ordinary hair spray will remove many ballpoint inks. For best results, test different methods on a hidden spot using ink from the same pen that caused the original stain. Ink formulas vary, and what will remove one may permanently set another.

*Mildew.* Launder with detergent and chlorine bleach whenever fabric and construction permit. In other instances, take your problem to a professional dry-cleaner, first identifying the stain for his guidance.

*Mud.* First allow to dry thoroughly and then brush lightly. Sometimes, this is all that will be needed. If a stain remains, launder when possible or shampoo with "dry" detergent suds, rinsing with clear water or a damp cloth.

*Salad dressing.* If non-washable fabric or carpet is involved, sponge with cool water and then shampoo with detergent suds. Finish by sponging with dry-cleaning solvent to remove any oily residue. If the fabric is washable, treat the oily stain with detergent paste or commercial spotting agent and launder as indicated.

*Soft drinks.* Sponge immediately with cool water or soak for 30 minutes if fabric and construction allow. Next, launder or shampoo with upholstery cleaner. Never neglect soft drink spills even if they are colorless. While perhaps invisible at first, many turn yellow with age or heat.

*Urine.* Accidents occur more frequently on carpeting than upholstery. Immediately sponge area with cool water. Then follow by shampooing with detergent suds, rinsing well. Urine is a difficult stain to remove once dry. Speed is your greatest ally.

## A FEW COMMONLY NEEDED REPAIRS

This section provides instructions for several simple home furnishings repairs that require few tools or supplies not ordinarily found in the home. While many others could have been selected that would be helpful in individual situations, these seem to be most needed when purchasing less-than-new home furnishings. Consult the references listed at the back of this book when specific repair problems arise that have not been covered in the text.

## Defective Light Bulb Socket

Table and floor lamps are often discarded because of defective sockets. In most cases, the contact points are worn and a new socket is needed. New sockets can be purchased in the electrical department of most hardware stores and the repair is simple:

1. Before beginning, unplug the lamp.
2. Remove the bulb.
3. Remove outer brass shell of socket from the cap by pressing near the switch button on the area marked "press."
4. Remove inner cardboard liner.
5. The socket itself now remains. Loosen the terminal screws releasing the two conductor wires. Remove the socket.
6. Replace the new socket, reassembling in reverse order. Generally the old cap will fit the new socket. Should you wish to replace the cap, untie the underwriter's knot, thread wires through the new cap, and retie the knot as shown in Chapter Seven.

## Damaged Frames with Plaster Ornament

Often the ornamental trim on an old mirror or picture frame requires a bit of repair before the piece can be hung with pride. While carved woodwork requires considerable woodworking ability, repairs to gilt frames are not exceedingly difficult. Before beginning work on the ornament, clean the frame thoroughly with soap and water. Plaster repairs will adhere better to a damp, clean surface. Mix patching plaster, available from paint or hardware stores, with sufficient water to create a dough-like consistency. Mound enough of this mixture over the damaged section to compensate for the missing trim. Mold to the approximate shape of the desired ornament with fingers while still damp. When dry, further shape the form with a sharp knife, finishing with fine sandpaper; repaint.

## Loose Knobs or Handles

Often the screws fastening knobs and handles become loose with age. There are several ways to rebuild the surrounding wood surfaces. Slivers of wood such as matchsticks or toothpicks can be used to compensate for the worn area. After placement, perhaps secured with a spot of glue, rethread the original screw. A string coated with liquid shellac wrapped around the original screw will also serve to shim up the worn area. A filler such as putty-type epoxy also builds up worn surfaces. However, after filling, thread the screw in place before the resin hardens or the insertion will be nearly impossible.

## Small Holes in Wicker Constructions

Repairing a hole in the cane section of a chair or sofa is easy. Buy a length of cane from a hobby supply or furniture repair shop and soak it in warm water until flexible. Trim any broken ends from the section to be repaired. Weave in the new strip of cane, concealing the new ends under the old cane. When the material has dried, glue in place using household cement. Secure with C-clamps to form a firm bond. Protect the cane surface with a layer of wax paper on each side; next place a board on top of each layer and clamp all together firmly.

Baskets can be repaired in a similar fashion by adapting the method of clamping to suit the situation. When working with stiffer wicker constructions, reweaving may be all that is needed to hold the replacements in position.

# 10

# budgeting
# for appliances
# and furnishings

Everyone wants to be a smart shopper and get full value for each dollar spent. But what a complicated business shopping is! We need to be informed consumers, aware of prices and quality of available goods, store reputations, and credit costs. To achieve long term satisfaction, we also need to be aware of our own values and goals. Finally, we must balance all these factors with our available resources. Admittedly, it takes time and practice to make wise decisions, but since we all make many purchases during our lifetime, our efforts will be repaid many times over.

## EVALUATE YOUR VALUES, GOALS, AND RESOURCES

When furnishing and equipping our homes, we must each decide which goals are most important, based upon our individual and family values. To achieve our goals, we must set them realistically, considering our total resources. While standard budgets may offer guidelines for income allocation, it is only after careful consideration of our own priorities and resources that an agreeable spending plan can evolve.

## Values and Goals

One family, placing a high value on economy, may furnish its home sparsely at first, while saving to buy more furniture in the future, avoiding credit costs. Another, valuing comfort and prestige, may immediately buy what is considered necessary for its way of life at the current rate of interest. Often we must resolve conflicting values within ourselves or among family members. When considering home furnishings, a family may value economy *and* comfort. Each must decide which values are most important in a given situation, then base realistic goals on this knowledge.

When determining your home furnishings needs, consider your life style and family composition. Don't inhibit the quality of family relationships by placing fragile furnishings in areas that demand greater care than can be reasonably expected at this stage in your family life cycle. In short, homes are for people and they should not hinder good relationships.

The family life cycle is an important consideration when setting goals. While some families do not follow the entire cycle and others may be at several stages at once, it still provides a convenient framework for evaluation of family needs. Whether a family is in the beginning, expanding, or contracting phase of this cycle has considerable influence in determining what furnishings and appliances will be needed in the home.

In general, the young family has far greater flexibility in this selection. Children generally bring not only a need for more space, furniture, and laborsaving appliances, but also a greater strain on family resources. The contracting family often seeks a smaller home or alternate housing in preparation for retirement. While greater freedom of choice returns, the prospect of lowered income and energy generally modifies this selection.

## Available Resources

Resources are the many assets available to help us achieve what we consider important. While money is certainly a vital resource, the quality of life depends on the full utilization of all available resources, material, human, and environmental. Material resources include money, goods, and community services. Our skills, knowledge, energy, interests, and attitudes are part of our human resources. A third form, seldom considered but nevertheless important when making family purchasing decisions, is environmental. The quality of air, land, and water is becoming increasingly important in our lives, and these resources have a direct bearing upon many of our decisions.

When buying for the home, we need to make decisions that will fulfill our needs and desires and yet be consistent with available resources. While all resources are limited in nature, in many instances they are also interchangeable. While as a family we may agree that the need for a dining table and chairs is immediate, the choices available to satisfy this need are many. If we have enough money, we may buy whatever pleases us. If not, we might buy on credit at extra cost, use a card table and chairs while saving for a new set, or perhaps buy and refinish an inexpensive but well built secondhand table and chairs. In the latter case, we would be substituting our time, energy, and skills in part for money. The wisdom of any of these decisions depends on family values and goals.

It is increasingly important to consider availability of time and energy when selecting home furnishings and appliances. A working mother may have very different values concerning furniture maintenance and laborsaving devices from a full-time homemaker. There is certainly a difference in need between the physically impaired and the unencumbered homemaker. The family with several pre-school children, the adult couple, or the elderly person living in a retirement home where meals are ordinarily taken in a dining room all have different time and energy resources. These variables should be considered when selecting furnishings and equipment.

## BECOME AN INFORMED CONSUMER

Knowledge of our needs, of prices and quality of available goods, store reputations, advertising techniques, and credit costs are all vital to successful purchasing. The more we know about merchandise, alternate sources of supply, and necessary installation or maintenance needs, the better we will be able to manage our shopping dollar.

### Consumer Information Sources

How can we become informed consumers? One way to learn about home furnishings and appliances is to read a variety of references, evaluating the advice in terms of its objectivity, validity, and application to our needs. Books are available which cover the field broadly or deal with such specific facets as lighting or appliance maintenance and repair. Many newspapers and magazines feature articles offering buying, maintenance, do-it-yourself repair or construction, and new product development information. Several consumer testing laboratories publish regular ratings of appliances and offer advice on the selection of other furnishings for the home in their monthly periodicals. We can also learn about specific merchandise characteristics and needs by reading advertisements, catalog descriptions, labels and hangtags, use and care manuals, installation instructions, and manufacturers' specification sheets.

Other sources of information are also available to the consumer; however, the advice offered may show varying degrees of expertise and impartiality. We can learn about quality and performance characteristics by talking to experienced salespeople, repairmen, and other consumers. Utility, university, and extension home economists as well as consumer specialists are impartial resources who can either provide the information you seek or direct you to another reliable source. Industry and trade associations who maintain consumer information or educational departments will usually answer any questions promptly. Performance standards, industry or governmental certification, and safety seals all tell us about the product, although we may need to do some initial research to determine the evaluating criteria.

After seeking product information and evaluating it in terms of our own needs, we must still compare available merchandise, prices, service, and terms offered in the market place. It is only after this step that we are ready to make our final purchasing decision.

### Credit Costs

If credit is to be used when making a purchase, additional consumer information is needed. Truth-in-lending legislation has gone far in clarifying the mysteries of credit costs. Varying forms of credit are available from finance companies, banks, credit unions, and retail stores. Regardless of the source or form, one thing is sure: any credit costs money. And in general, the longer you take to pay for a purchase, the higher the cost.

To figure the dollar cost of using any credit plan, you need to know: the trade-in allowance, if any; amount of down payment; any additional charges such as insurance; amount of regular payments; number of payments; and the cash price.  To calculate:

List the down payment cost $\qquad$ \$ _____

Add trade-in allowance, if any + \$ _____

Add any additional charges or
   insurance, if any + \$ _____

Add the amount of regular payments
   multiplied by the number required:

  \$_____ x _____ = + \$ _____
   (amount)   (no. required)

        **TOTAL PRICE YOU WILL PAY** \$ _____

Subtract cash price − \$ _____

        **TOTAL COST OF CREDIT** \$ _____

### Installation, Service, and Maintenance Costs

When considering how any purchase will fit into your budget at a given time, weigh not only the initial price and any credit costs, but also delivery, installation, operating, and service or maintenance expense.  In some cases, appliance installation costs can equal the original purchase price.  When reupholstering a sofa, the choice of a delicate fabric needing professional cleaning will add substantially more to household expense than a washable vinyl covering.  As another alternative, a removable slipcover would cut initial labor costs, clean inexpensively in a self-service dry-cleaning machine, yet provide the warmth of a conventional fabric lacking in the plastic covering.

In areas where both gas and electricity are available, a comparison of utility costs is helpful when deciding which central heating system, clothes dryer, water heater, or range to buy.  Investigate both the all-gas and electric as well as the standard utility rates.  In addition, learn the cost of any utility installation, additional electric branch circuits or increased service entrance capacity, and any necessary construction costs or permits.  Check to see if free repair and adjustment services are offered by either utility, comparing the hourly charge for a service-man's time for these same repairs.

Gas is metered in cubic feet and electricity in kilowatt hours.  In order to convert these terms to a common factor for comparison, we often evaluate their production of heat in British Thermal Units (BTU).

---

**FUEL COST COMPARISON: NATURAL GAS AND ELECTRICITY**

*Equivalents:*

1 therm = 100,000 BTU

1 cubic foot natural gas = 1,000 BTU

1 kilowatt hour (KWH) electricity = 3,412 BTU

*To convert therms to KWH:*

$$\frac{\text{(No. of therms)} \times 100,000}{3,412} = \text{KWH}$$

---

In comparing the operating costs, find out the relative thermal efficiencies for each appliance and the local applicable residential rate from both your gas and electric utilities. While cost of equipment and operational expenses are not the only factors involved in your appliance selection, both should be weighed carefully before arriving at a final decision.

## TAKE ADVANTAGE OF SALES

The key to success here is to take advantage of rather than be taken by sales. Impulse buying is rarely a good idea. Often a huge reduction in a sofa or chair may falsely lead us to spend more than our budget can stand. Don't overspend because a purchase is such a "bargain." Be consistent with your resources.

Home furnishings and appliance sales come in many guises. We find seasonal sales that usually occur just before new stock arrives; private sales, held for regular customers a few days prior to a general announcement; closeout sales; even old-fashioned dollar days. Special purchase and anniversary sales frequently feature some sub-standard merchandise bought specially for the sale. Inspect carefully before purchasing. In general, sales are held to:

Clear out older merchandise, making room for new goods.

Sell surplus or shopworn goods.

Encourage new customers to visit a store.

Introduce new products to customers.

Liquidate an entire store inventory in cases of bankruptcy or
  business closure.

When we understand the reason for a specific sale, we are better able to
shop wisely and avoid the usual pitfalls.

Nothing can take the place of sound consumer knowledge. It is
not unusual for certain stores to inflate price tags just prior to a
markdown. Retailers' ads sometimes provide a clue to the dependability
of a sale. When stores advertise that items are "reduced from our
regular price," the savings are probably authentic. However, be wary
of such claims as "half our competitor's price." When sale merchandise
is advertised as "discontinued," be sure that parts will be available
when repairs are necessary and that the style is suitable to your family
situation.

True bargains are goods needed or desired in their own right (not
simply because they are on sale) that represent an actual savings over
the regular price. When buying shopworn or damaged goods, consider
necessary cleaning and repair costs as part of the total price. These
extras can sometimes cancel the entire savings.

Timing your purchases to coincide with the nationally organized
pattern that retail stores usually follow when setting up home furnishings and appliance sales or special promotions can save you money.
Such information is especially valuable when planning for regularly
occurring purchases, such as linens or major expenditures, that are not
of an emergency nature. In addition to these traditional promotions,
other special sales occur on a local basis. It is always well to check the
store merchandising manager for exact sale periods.

## FILE INFORMATION FOR FUTURE USE

Remember that managing your home furnishings and equipment
dollar does not end with purchasing. A file that helps you to
organize necessary household records and instructions should be set
up immediately following your first purchase. Collect any invoices,

## SHOPPING CALENDAR

*Sales and special promotions*

| January | February | March |
|---------|----------|-------|
| White goods, small appliances, furniture, store-wide clearances | Matresses, rugs, furniture and home furnishings, housewares, curtains, glassware, china | Housewares, china, silver |

| April | May | June |
|-------|-----|------|
| Spring cleaning supplies, paints, housewares, outdoor furniture | White goods, soap, cleaning aids, air conditioners, fans, outdoor furniture | Rug cleaning supplies, lumber refrigerators, fabrics |

| July | August | September |
|------|--------|----------|
| Floor coverings, refrigerators, washing machines, furniture | Furniture, curtains, paint, hardware, white goods, fall fabrics | Home furnishings, china, glassware, accessories |

| October | November | December |
|---------|----------|----------|
| Home furnishings | Blankets, china, glassware, table linens, home furnishings | Christmas promotions |

guarantees, repair information, user's manuals and other instructions needed for proper care and maintenance of furnishings and household equipment. Such an information file is of an individual nature and should be designed to serve your particular situation.

The file might contain a stain removal chart, laundering directions for those items not marked with permanent care labels, furniture care techniques, and perhaps even the shopping calendar. Record the purchase of any goods accompanied by a guarantee or warranty. The exact dates of purchase will expedite service during this period. A form similar to the record shown in this section can help to organize such information and might appropriately be attached to a folder holding related invoices and guarantees for easy reference.

| YOUR EQUIPMENT RECORD | | | |
|---|---|---|---|
| | *Date Purchased* | *Where Purchased* | *Warranty Expiration Date* | *For Service Call* |
| Washer | | | |
| Dryer | | | |
| Refrigerator | | | |
| Freezer | | | |
| Range | | | |
| Dishwasher | | | |
| Air conditioner | | | |
| Television | | | |
| Food waste disposer | | | |
| Vacuum cleaner | | | |
| Stereo | | | |
| Other | | | |

# references

Anderson, Edwin P. *Home Appliance Servicing.* Indianapolis: Theodore Audel, 1971.

Beedell, Suzanne. *Restoring Junk.* London: Macdonald, 1970.

Berger, Robert. *All About Antiquing and Restoring Furniture.* New York: Hawthorn Books, 1971.

*Better Homes and Gardens Handyman's Book.* Des Moines, Iowa: Meredith Corporation, 1972.

Campbell, Robert and H. H. Mager. *How to Work with Tools and Wood.* New York: Simon and Schuster, 1972.

Carter, Myrtle. "Re-upholstering a Chair at Home." *Extension Bulletin 406,* Cooperative Extension Service, Washington State University, Pullman, 1967.

Cassiday, Bruce. *The New Practical Home Repair for Women.* New York: Taplinger, 1972.

Curry, Barbara A. *Okay, I'll Do It Myself!* New York: Random House, 1971.

Dickerson, Lila B. "Making Slip Covers." *Extension Bulletin 480,* Cooperative Extension Service, Washington State University, Pullman, 1962.

Endacott, G. W. *Woodworking and Furniture Making for the Home.* New York: Drake, 1972.

Flitman, Malcolm. *Upholstering.* New York: Drake, 1972.

Gibbia, S. W. *Wood Finishing and Refinishing.* New York: Van Nostrand Reinhold, 1971.

Haywood, Charles H. *The Complete Book for Woodwork.* New York: Drake, 1972.

    *The Complete Handyman.* New York: Drake, 1969.

    *Staining and Polishing.* New York: Drake, 1972.

Hertzberg, Robert. *Handyman's Electrical Repairs.* New York: Arco, 1959.

Howes, C. *Practical Upholstery,* New York: Drake, 1971.

Kinney, Ralph Parsons. *The Complete Book of Furniture Repair and Refinishing.* New York: Charles Scribner's Sons, 1971.

*Manual of Home Repairs, Remodeling and Maintenance.* New York: Fawcett, 1969.

Moore, Alma Chesnut. *How to Clean Everything.* New York: Simon and Schuster, 1960.

Patton, Albert B. and Clarence L. Vaugh. *Furniture: Furniture Finishing, Decoration and Patching.* New York: Drake, 1970.

Ratcliff, Rosemary. *Refurbishing Antiques.* Chicago: Henry Regnery, 1971.

Schuler, Stanley. *How to Fix Almost Everything.* New York: Simon and Schuster, 1970.

Thames, Gena. "Furniture Restoration." *Extension Bulletin 548,* Cooperative Extension Service, Washington State University, Pullman, 1971.

"Reupholstering Chairs with Foam Rubber." *Extension Bulletin 554,* Cooperative Extension Service, Washington State University, Pullman, 1970.

Wright, Veva Penick. *Pamper Your Possessions.* Barre, Mass. Barre, 1972.

# index

# acknowledgements

Vacuum cleaner drawings from photographs courtesy of the Hoover Company.

Veneer finish illustration taken from the Money Management Institute booklet titled <u>Your Home Furnishings Dollar</u> printed by the Money Management Institute of Household Finance Corporation, Prudential Plaza, Chicago, Illinois 60601.